Traveling in
Mark Twain

Richard Bridgman

Traveling in Mark Twain

University of California Press

Berkeley   Los Angeles   London

University of California Press
Berkeley and Los Angeles, California

University of California Press, Ltd.
London, England

© 1987 by
The Regents of the University of California

Library of Congress Cataloging-in-Publication Data

Bridgman, Richard.
  Traveling in Mark Twain.
    1. Twain, Mark, 1835–1910—Knowledge—Geography.
2. Twain, Mark, 1835–1910—Journeys.   3. Travel in
literature.   4. Voyages and travels.   I. Title.
PS1342.G4B75   1987   818'.409   86–25037
ISBN 0–520–05952–2 (alk. paper)

Printed in the United States of America
1 2 3 4 5 6 7 8 9

*In memory of Frederick Anderson
and Joseph M. Backus*

Acknowledgments

By giving me the benefit of their individual perspectives and expertise, four colleagues and friends—Robert Hirst, George Starr, Frederick Crews, and Stephanie Fay—measurably improved this essay. The University of California assisted the project by its maintenance of the Mark Twain Papers in the Bancroft Library and by supplying sabbatical free time as well as those funds allocated by the Berkeley Academic Senate Committee on Research. For all this personal and institutional support, once more, my gratitude.

Abbreviations

Whenever possible in the text, I have indicated the source of a quotation parenthetically by an abbreviation or short title and the page number. Other references and extensions of the point are footnoted.

ET&S1   Twain, Mark. *Early Tales & Sketches*. Volume 1, 1851–1864. Edited by Edgar M. Branch and Robert H. Hirst. Berkeley: University of California Press, 1979.

ET&S2   Twain, Mark. *Early Tales & Sketches*. Volume 2, 1864–1865. Edited by Edgar M. Branch and Robert H. Hirst. Berkeley: University of California Press, 1981.

FE   Twain, Mark. *Following the Equator: A Journey around the World*. Hartford, Connecticut: American Publishing Company, 1897.

IA   Twain, Mark. *The Innocents Abroad; or, The New Pilgrims' Progress*. Hartford, Connecticut: American Publishing Company, 1869.

LLMT   Twain, Mark. *The Love Letters of Mark Twain*. Edited by Dixon Wecter. New York: Harper and Brothers, 1949.

LOM   Twain, Mark. *Life on the Mississippi*. With an introduction by Edward Wagenknecht and a number of previously suppressed passages [from the Pierpont Morgan Library holographic manuscript], now printed for the first time and edited with a note by Willis Wager. New York: Limited Editions Club, 1944.

MSM Twain, Mark. *The Mysterious Stranger Manuscripts*. Edited by William M. Gibson. Berkeley: University of California Press, 1969.

MTB Paine, Albert Bigelow. *Mark Twain: A Biography*. 3 vols., pages numbered continuously. New York: Harper and Brothers, 1912.

MTBus *Mark Twain, Business Man*. Edited by Samuel C. Webster. Boston: Little, Brown and Company, 1946.

MTHHR *Mark Twain's Correspondence with Henry Huttleston Rogers, 1893–1909*. Edited by Lewis Leary. Berkeley: University of California Press, 1969.

MTHL *Mark Twain–Howells Letters*. 2 vols. Edited by Henry Nash Smith and William M. Gibson. Cambridge: Harvard University Press, 1960.

MTL *Mark Twain's Letters*. 2 vols. Edited by Albert Bigelow Paine. New York: Harper and Brothers, 1917.

MTLP *Mark Twain's Letters to His Publishers, 1867–1894*. Edited by Hamlin Hill. Berkeley: University of California Press, 1967.

MTN *Mark Twain's Notebook*. Edited by Albert Bigelow Paine. New York: Harper and Brothers, 1935.

MTP Mark Twain Papers, Bancroft Library, University of California, Berkeley.

MTSp *Mark Twain's Speeches*. With an introduction by Albert Bigelow Paine. New York: Harper and Brothers, 1923.

N&J1   *Mark Twain's Notebooks & Journals.* Volume I, 1855–1873. Edited by Frederick Anderson, Michael B. Frank, and Kenneth M. Sanderson. Berkeley: University of California Press, 1975.

N&J2   *Mark Twain's Notebooks & Journals.* Volume 2, 1877–1883. Edited by Frederick Anderson, Lin Salamo, and Bernard L. Stein. Berkeley: University of California Press, 1975.

N&J3   *Mark Twain's Notebooks & Journals.* Volume 3, 1883–1891. Edited by Robert Pack Browning, Michael B. Frank, and Lin Salamo. Berkeley: University of California Press, 1979.

RI   Twain, Mark. *Roughing It.* With an introduction and explanatory notes by Franklin R. Rogers. Berkeley: University of California Press, 1972.

S&B   *Mark Twain's Satires & Burlesques.* Edited by Franklin R. Rogers. Berkeley: University of California Press, 1967.

TA   Twain, Mark. *A Tramp Abroad.* Hartford, Connecticut: American Publishing Company, 1880.

TS   Twain, Mark. *The Adventures of Tom Sawyer.* Foreword and notes by John C. Gerber. Text established by Paul Baender. Berkeley: University of California Press, 1982.

WIM   Twain, Mark. *What Is Man? and Other Philosophical Writings.* Edited by Paul Baender. Berkeley: University of California Press, 1973.

WWD   *Mark Twain's Which Was The Dream? and Other Symbolic Writings of the Later Years.* Edited by John S. Tuckey. Berkeley: University of California Press, 1967.

1

Change was a conspicuous feature of Mark Twain's emphatically American life. Energetic, impatient, fidgety, invariably pursuing a host of projects, many of them not literary, he was constantly on the move. That he should have gravitated to travel writing now seems inevitable. He early discovered that the genre afforded him a license to react to whatever caught his fancy and be paid for it. His 1866 contract with the *Alta California* newspaper stipulated that he was to compose travel letters "on such subjects and from such places as will best suit him."[1] It was an opportunity he seized with enthusiasm, and before he gave it up, he had produced numerous travel letters and essays, as well as five full-length travel books.

Travel writing not only encouraged Mark Twain to comment on striking aspects of the world—no small gift for an easily bored moralist—but it also permitted him to use his special literary gifts, which displayed themselves best in the short bursts of pointed observations, anecdotes, episodes, and tales. He could examine the diversity of the world without worrying overmuch about such matters as consistency or transitions, for the travel account proved capable of absorbing any improvisation he might conceive. "Jim Baker's Bluejay Yarn," which takes place in the Sierra, ended up in an account of a European walking tour, and a tale

1. Ivan Benson, *Mark Twain's Western Years* (Stanford, 1938), 152.

laid in a Munich morgue is told during a trip down the Mississippi.

Mark Twain's friend Charles Dudley Warner, who collaborated with Twain on *The Gilded Age,* opened a travel volume of his own by underlining the gratifying irresponsibility available in the form: "Let us not be under the misapprehension that we are set any task other than that of sauntering where it pleases us."[2] Still, while the journey produced variety, it also conferred an elemental order on the random experiences. This proved to be especially helpful and even liberating for Twain. Within limits, he was an unusually disciplined writer, capable of unparalleled clarity and precision in his prose. But in spite of his earnest efforts to outline his work in advance and to revise it afterwards, few would argue on behalf of his narrative structures. It seems no coincidence that Twain received his training as a professional writer on newspapers and that he read them insatiably all his life, for a newspaper provides an experience analogous to that available in a travel narrative: a cornucopia of facts, stories, and commentaries, minimally linked at best and without any synthesizing conclusion.[3] In a travel account, though, Twain could rely on the sequence of the journey itself to provide at least a simulacrum of coherence for his materials. However arbitrary or disproportionate the stages of the journey might be, they still lay along a central organizational spine that started somewhere, moved linearly, and ended somewhere else.

Although Mark Twain could render the immediate moment brilliantly, he was tormented all his life because he

2. Charles Dudley Warner, *Saunterings* (1872; Boston, 1879), xii.

3. For a brief review of Twain's relationship to newspapers, see Louis J. Budd, *Our Mark Twain: The Making of His Public Personality* (Philadelphia, 1983), 97–99.

could not make the world he observed conform to that model transmitted to him in his youth; even after he had scornfully discarded Hannibal's tenets, the world remained askew. Each of his rebukes of human behavior, whether direct or satiric, and each of his disclosures of hypocrisy and imposture contributed to its destabilization. Lacking a sense of a coherent universe, he found it difficult to produce a unified narrative. Or if he produced one, it was liable to be based on a mechanical manipulation of relationships as in *The Prince and the Pauper,* or on a plot furnished by history as in *Joan of Arc.* Paradoxically, chaotic jumbles like *A Connecticut Yankee* and *Pudd'nhead Wilson,* in spite of their formal problems, are much more interesting because in them Twain's deeper preoccupations are contesting for control of the narrative. As he probed beneath conventional surfaces, contradictions emerged that he could not reconcile in a consistently developed plot. Although a similar problem occurred in the travel narratives, there it was hardly noticeable, so tolerant was the genre of diversity. One need have neither a coherent worldview nor even a particular end in mind to write a travel book. All that the form demanded Twain had in abundance: curiosity, a reactive intelligence, and stamina.

Travel itself had powerful attractions for a skeptical intelligence like Twain's. Its formal displacements generated the very situations that produce humor: values clashed, perspectives underwent abrupt shifts, and around the next corner, surprise. Hungry for reality, Twain once noted on the back of an envelope: "I like history, biography, travels, curious facts and strange happenings and science. And I detest novels, poetry and theology" (*MTB,* 512). Like most humorists, who by definition have a professional interest in disparities, Twain was a deeply serious person faced with a world whose ostensible order remained tantalizingly elusive for him. In his travel books one can often listen to him thinking out loud about problems like filth or cowardice, then abruptly "solving" them by an explosive joke. If at times his thoughts turned opaque or confused, that was the price of independent reflection.

Those hazy moments in his travels came when Mark Twain encountered or thought of something that was sufficiently compelling for him to want to record it; yet when he translated it onto the page, it remained problematic, for his conscious mind had not yet mastered it. Such puzzling junctures, although often overlooked, can be importantly revealing because they emerge from those hidden transactions that the intuition conducts with the unconscious. As the looseness of the travel account provided a particularly receptive vehicle for such materials, this essay is obliged to think as much about psychological patterns as geographical ones. Here, when I can, I start at certain provocative or enigmatic points and try to follow their threads into the labyrinth of Twain's mind. The stony faces in the Parthenon grass, the Greeley letter, the dead volcano of Haleakala, the thrashing of Conrad Wiegand, the sketch of the Jungfrau, the wreck of the *Duncan Dunbar,* the fruit of what Twain called the dorian, and the transvestite military surgeon are among these symbolic nodes. As Twain felt compelled to include them, I have undertaken to consider why he did so. At times, though, I can only point silently at their oddness.

Obscure observations in Twain's travel books do not invariably have subterranean origins. On occasion a mechanical lapse furnishes the explanation. Consider, for example, this complete paragraph from *A Tramp Abroad:* "I was taught a lesson in political economy in Frankfurt. I had brought from home a box containing a thousand very cheap cigars. By way of experiment, I stepped into a little shop in a queer old back street, took four gaily decorated boxes of wax matches and three cigars, and laid down a silver piece worth 48 cents. The man gave me 43 cents change" (18).

What was the "lesson in political economy" being illustrated? Given the *Tramp* text alone, one can only guess. As it turns out, the word *political* is misleading. The original notebook entry shows that Twain meant something like "comparative" here: "Bought 2 cigars & 4 boxes fancy matches—gave 48 cent piece and got 42½ cents change. Shant import any more cheap cigars into Germany for economy's sake" (*N&J2*, 89).

If Twain's wife, friends, and editors who read the manuscript before publication as well as his audience failed to object to the ambiguities of such moments, it was apparently because the brilliant, ongoing flood of language and humor reconciled them to missing the point of an anecdote from time to time. The details of Twain's prose simply didn't matter as long as one received an adequate measure of entertainment.

For Mrs. Clemens, the one exception was overt vulgarity. During Mark Twain's first years as a lecturer, he had been less inhibited than he became after his marriage and international success. But even in the West there had been regular complaints about his "low" language and humor. Bret Harte identified Twain's faults as "crudeness, coarseness, and an occasional Panurge-like plainness of statement." In reviewing a stage performance, the *San Francisco Chronicle* found some of Twain's jokes "so nearly improper—not to say coarse—that they could not be heartily laughed at by ladies." The *San Francisco Evening Bulletin* thought his humor "audacious" and "sometimes verging on coarseness."[4] Later, though, motivated by a desire for acceptance and material success, Twain submitted to the moderating influence of friends like Howells and his wife Livy. But before selected audiences he continued to play the role of the knowing male, as when he wrote *1601* or delivered "Some

4. All quotations are taken from Paul Fatout, *Mark Twain on the Lecture Circuit* (Bloomington, Ind., 1960), 41, 60.

Thoughts on the Science of Onanism" to the Stomach Club of Paris in 1879. Like "The King's Camelopard" in *Huckleberry Finn,* these were performances to which ladies and children were not admitted. Of the "Onanism" speech, A. B. Paine noted that it "has obtained a wide celebrity among the clubs of the world, though no line of it, or even its title, has ever found its way into published literature" (*MTB,* 643).

Even after Mark Twain had publicly reformed, it still amused him to introduce forbidden matter into his work. Sometimes it was to make a point that only the experienced would understand. At other times it was a form of teasing play on his part. A domestic example comes to mind. In a letter Clemens wrote to his sister-in-law in 1871, he referred to his new son, Langdon: "The baby's weight has increased to 7½ pounds & his personal comeliness in proportion. I feel that I can say without exaggeration that he is humping himself." Mrs. Clemens crossed out "humping" and wrote: "Our little boy never humps. Livy." Clemens then put "humping" back in again, this time in purple ink (*MTBus,* 11).

How shall we understand Livy's intervention? One meaning of *to hump oneself* is "to hurry," to gather oneself together to project oneself forward, as when Huck cries, "Git up and hump yourself, Jim! There ain't a minute to lose. They're after us!" (chap. 11). Another, related, sense of the term is "to work hard," as Clemens used it in a letter to Charles Dudley Warner when Livy was nursing the infant Susy but producing insufficient milk. Susy, Clemens wrote, "keeps one cow 'humping herself'" (*LLMT,* 174). But why should those senses of the idiom require censorship and denial, however lighthearted? That her baby is growing rapidly is one of the proudest maternal claims.

The probable explanation is that *humping* also has irregular connotations. Among its other meanings, *to hump* is to engage in sexual intercourse. Not that Clemens meant that his baby was necessarily doing something sexual (although infantile erections might have been a matter of parental observation and comment). Rather, he seems to have been taking pleasure in using a slang term that possessed a secondary, roughneck, connotation, like that suggested in an 1891 notebook where he set down a line in quotation marks, as if it had been overheard: "'By the humping jumping J——s what the h——l is that to you?'"[5]

It is not likely that Livy "knew" what "humping" meant, unless Clemens had informed her in their domestic intimacies, but she certainly sensed its vulgarity. Her editing must have derived, then, from her awareness of her husband's command of coarse language and his general mischievousness. Intuiting the word's suggestiveness, she emphatically announced that "our little boy never humps," no doubt doubling her husband's amusement. Whether she herself appreciated the humor of that assertion, we don't know. But this kind of suggestive joking is altogether consistent with Mark Twain's habits and temperament, and in *Following the Equator* we shall see analogous moments in connection with the words *lingam* and *dorian*.

The "humping" example admittedly remains ambiguous, and in fact a penumbra of uncertainty frequently obscures Mark Twain's intentions at such moments. Normally one prefers to offer examples where research and thought have managed to illuminate a crux, but sometimes in Twain's writings that is not possible. Enigmatic presences call out for attention, obliging one repeatedly to ask what motivated the telling of that particular anecdote in just that way? What did Mark Twain think he was communicating by its inclusion? Should the anecdote be regarded as mere filler, or has some trivial carelessness, as in the transfer of the

5. Notebook no. 31 (Aug. 31, 1891–July 4, 1892), 1, *MTP*.

notebook entry on the purchase of cigars in Frankfurt, obscured an otherwise straightforward meaning? Or does the significance lie hidden in Twain's psyche, unrecognized even by him? The legitimacy of the questions remains even in the absence of decisive answers. Loose ends are inevitable. They signify a reality larger than the one that has thus far been contained.

A Tramp Abroad contains an anecdote with the ambiguous features I have been speaking about. It begins as Mark Twain discovers that German opera audiences applaud at the end of an act, rather than immediately following an aria. Twain says that he felt "unspeakably uncomfortable in the solemn dead silences" that ensued after a performer's "tremendous outpourings of his feelings" (95). That sensation of acute psychological discomfort in turn reminded him how he had felt when as a boy of ten he made his first trip ever aboard a Mississippi steamboat. He recalled having "gone to bed with his head filled with impending snaggings, and explosions, and conflagrations, and sudden death." Later he had abruptly risen from his bunk, wearing only a "brief shirt," and had run to the ladies' saloon, where he cried out, "Fire fire!" The women present, who were quietly knitting, greeted this hysteria with a calmness that thoroughly humiliated the impressionable boy.

As recorded, the behavior in the episode is perplexing. We do not know why the women were not at least initially alarmed by the boy's startling cries, nor do we learn why a boy should necessarily be haunted by images of incipient disaster aboard a riverboat. We do know, however, that in Mark Twain's writing a source of a male's shame often involved his being obliged to appear unwillingly before females in an exposed condition—nude like Hank Morgan when he was first brought to King Arthur's court or, as here, "encased in a quite short shirt" (95–96). Furthermore, when we return to the manuscript of this episode, we find that originally when the boy appeared, "all those ladies looked sweetly up & blushed" until at last an old lady "said, gently—'What you *want,* on that thing, is a *fringe, you know!*'" With that, the boy gasped for breath, turned, and "crept humbly away in a stooping attitude."[6] In the printed version, all that remains of this account is an off-hand reference to the boy's brief shirt and his excruciating embarrassment, with no certain connection between them.

Further, given Twain's persistent anxieties as a cub pilot as well as his having witnessed the suffering and death of his brother following a steamboat explosion, we would not be wrong, I think, to draw the obvious psychological con-clusions to account for the awkward appearance of this story in the *Tramp.* Since neither that biographical informa-tion nor the earlier draft of the story with its genital focus is available to a reader of the book, however, the anecdote as told has no significance beyond whatever crude amusement one might derive from the boy's discomfiture.

It is worth emphasizing, though, that Mark Twain reached this account of a boyhood trauma by an associative bridge, for the mechanisms of association often liberated Twain's imagination. Here the silence of the German audi-ence after an operatic aria connected in his mind with the silence that followed the arrival of the overwrought boy, be-cause the two silences generated similar feelings of psycho-logical distress. The movements of the consciousness Twain was dramatizing might seem arbitrary viewed from the outside—how *did* one get from a German concert hall to a Mississippi riverboat?—but become comprehensibly re-lated with the testimony about the similar emotional states.

The organic quirkiness of human thought was per-petually interesting to Mark Twain. He early recognized

6. Photostat of ms. of the *Tramp,* Box 5, no. 10, pp. 306–9, *MTP.*

the essential discursiveness of his mind and in his first years on the lecture platform learned to exploit a subjective looseness in his discourse. A reviewer in 1867 observed: "The scheme of the lecturer appeared to be to employ the various facts he had gathered as bases upon which to build fanciful illustrations of character, which were furthermore embellished with a multitude of fantastic anecdotes and personal reminiscences. The frequent incongruities of the narration—evidently intentional—made it all the more diverting, and the artifice of its partial incoherence was so cleverly contrived as to intensify the amusement of the audience, while leaving them for the most part in ignorance of the means employed" (*ET&S1*, 56). Twain eventually realized that such apparent randomness represented his best understanding of how the mind operates. In *Roughing It,* for example, after pausing to remark that a particular subject had reminded him of yet another, which he would discuss forthwith, Twain added that he would normally apologize for such a digression, except that "I digress constantly anyhow" (318). That was true, and the textual histories of his travel books in particular testify to how casually they were composed. Twain could add, drop, or rearrange his materials without any appreciable effect on the whole. Elements migrated readily from book to book, so accommodating was the genre.

The travel books also exhibit instances of undistinguished digression. The commercial need for a volume of a specific size would sometimes force Twain to produce additional pages. One convenient means he found for generating material was to rely mechanically on associative sequences. In the *Tramp,* Twain remarks that everywhere in the city of Lucerne, Switzerland, were images of the lion of Lucerne for sale. The giant original had been carved into the face of a cliff to honor the Swiss guards slain while de-

fending Louis XVI. These lion images furnished the cue
for Twain first to reflect on the condition of martyrs in general, then to ruminate specifically on Mary Queen of Scots
and Marie Antoinette. Returning then to the ubiquitous
replicas of the lion, his mind next veered off along another
associative line involving other wooden carvings he had
seen in Lucerne. In particular he considered those used as
ornamentation on clocks, which led him to cuckoo clocks
and then inevitably to their sound, which he said was so
hateful that he had once sent a cuckoo clock as a gift to im-
pair the mind of a person he disliked. He added that he had
considered presenting a cuckoo clock to a certain book reviewer but had decided it would be useless, for "I couldn't
injure his mind" (263). With that triumphantly dismis-
sive remark, he concluded this section of his associative
mosaic—but not before he had managed to increase sub-
stantially the pile of manuscript pages.

At its best, such casualness was not a mark of self-indul-
gence. To render his understanding of the workings of the
mind more accurately, Mark Twain learned to use the sub-
surface logic of both associations and dreams. A. B. Paine
recalled that when Twain was dictating his autobiographical
reminiscences in his last years, "We never knew what he
was going to talk about, and it was seldom that *he* knew
until the moment of beginning; then he went drifting
among episodes, incidents, and periods in his irresponsible
fashion; the fashion of table-conversation, as he said, the
methodless method of the human mind" (*MTB,* 1268). But
well before the dictations, the travel book had empowered
Twain to follow the vagaries of his thought. Although
from one point of view, then, one might well say of the
Tramp that "nothing holds the book together except the
binding," in fact however disparate the materials, they do
unmistakably emerge from a single mind of marked char-

acteristics through which flow related themes that often discover their own coherence in the writing.[7] For Twain, X might be connected to F instead of to Y; and although in deference to social norms of composition F might be denied entrance to his page, Twain preferred to record it when he had the license to do so, for however unseemly it might appear, it best represented the relation of ideas that he actually experienced.

Mark Twain found another means of securing that license for naturalness by shifting responsibility for such seemingly anarchistic discourse to an untutored narrator like Huck Finn, author of Twain's greatest travel book. In *Roughing It,* the intoxicated Jim Blaine was another such narrator, who undertook to tell the story of his grandfather's old ram. After making its appearance in the opening sentences, that ram disappeared into the thickets of Blaine's mind, never to emerge again. Yet the story is as formally satisfying as any Mark Twain ever told, beginning with an observation that proves prophetic, both for the old ram and for human life—"I don't reckon them times will ever come again"—and ending with reflections on the mortality of a man seized by the machinery of a carpet factory and woven into a rug, a casualty of modern technology effectively assuring that indeed them times never would come again (344).

In his brilliant associative sequences Mark Twain carried out pioneering surveys of the inner landscape and discovered there harmonies other than any he had ever been taught governed existence. Meanwhile, though, Twain's geographical travels brought him little positive enlightenment. Everywhere, whether observing European civilization as a young adult in *The Innocents Abroad* or that of In-

7. Everett Emerson, *The Authentic Mark Twain: A Literary Biography of Samuel L. Clemens* (Philadelphia, 1984), 104.

dia as a man in his sixties in *Following the Equator,* he found life painful, cruel, and fundamentally absurd. While this stimulated his humor, which in turn vented off portions of his indignation, Twain's persistent problem was that he saw clearly enough what was wrong but could find no substitute for the ramshackle systems he was mocking—not in other cultures, or in himself.

For a long time Mark Twain's extraordinary energy overrode his revulsion, and his humor exploded away the contradictions. Eventually, though, the cumulative weight of his disillusionments proved too much even for him, so that near the end of his life his literary travels were no longer in this world. He could endure existence imaginatively only by supposing that it was no more than a bubble, an illusion, a very bad dream. In a sense this was true, for as his books testify, he had always been traveling in his mind.

2

The Innocents Abroad, Mark Twain's first travel book, which consolidated his fame and which has sustained its popularity, was on the surface his most conventional. Following a fixed itinerary, the tour ship, the *Quaker City,* took him along familiar touristic routes, ones so familiar, in fact, that earlier accounts of these standard sights became the targets of his mockery. Much of the book is a high-spirited, confident, and satirically inventive performance.

But there is another, more troubled, voice heard in it too. In the preface Mark Twain calls the *Quaker City* excursion "a pic-nic," and on the opening page, "a picnic on a gigantic scale" (v, 19). Americans do characteristically start off on trips, parties, marriages, careers, and wars in a state of unbounded optimism, something Melville knew when he described the green troops of the Union "gayly" marching off to the first battle of Bull Run as if it were a "picnic party in the May."[1] But irony is always waiting in the wings, and for all Mark Twain's festive expectations, the *Quaker City* tour proved to be dominated by "many elderly people" (32). By the time the pilgrims returned home, Mark Twain played indignantly on that motif. The trip turned out to have been a "picnic of patriarchs." Three-fourths of the "passengers were between forty and seventy years of age! There was a picnic crowd for you!" (644).

1. "The March into Virginia," in *Collected Poems of Herman Melville,* ed. Howard P. Vincent (Chicago, 1947), 10–11.

The Innocents Abroad records multiple betrayals, beginning with the composition of the group with which Mark Twain signed on so expectantly. Worse, though, the world itself that he went to see for the first time turned out to be largely a sham, the nature of which had been meretriciously falsified by the travelers who had preceded him as well as by the guides on the spot. If the book begins in an expectant mood, or no worse than a calmly ironic one, it ends weary, rancorous, and exhausted. There were a number of reasons for this negative tone. Mark Twain had tired of expanding and revising his original newspaper letters for the book, so he composed the second half more cursorily and with his exasperation closer to the surface. That exasperation centered on the pious, middle-aged Christian party in whose company he traveled, and it was heightened by plain fatigue from sightseeing. The whole party became "surfeited with sights" (582). Much more dispiriting than this, though, Europe, our old home, had proved to be decadent, and over the Middle Eastern cradle of civilization and spiritual resurrection, flies swarmed. If America was coarse and violent, the older worlds were deceitful, violent, and degraded.

Everywhere Mark Twain went on this trip, his attention was engrossed by imprisonment, torture, mutilation, and corpses. In effect, the tour led him to misery. Venal and idiotic guides took him deliberately to celebrated sites of suffering. Catholic art in particular was appalling to Twain, both in subject matter and in condition. Its subjects were martyred saints, skewered and writhing in pain, or the crucified Savior himself, hands mutilated, side pierced, body scourged and streaming with blood. And the paintings themselves were faded, patchy, cracked. Even at the *Quaker City*'s first stop in the Azores, the cathedral could offer only "a swarm of rusty, dusty, battered apostles" who had suffered various kinds of damage, such as the loss of an eye, fingers gone, or "not enough nose left to blow" (57). Later, at Notre-Dame de Paris, Twain again observed a facade that was "clustered thick with stony, mutilated saints" (130).

The classical gods had suffered similar indignities— Cupid was noseless, Jupiter was missing an eye, Venus had "a fly-blister on her breast" (167). Even the most famous depiction, Leonardo's *Last Supper,* proved to be "battered and scarred . . . stained and discolored by time" (190). But even though the pictorial representations of Christianity were monotonously conventional and in bad shape, the tourists still praised them as if they were perfect. The authenticity of religion, always a central issue for Mark Twain, rested for the moment on surfaces. The deeper problem might merely be that Old World Catholic corruption was in league with New World fatuity.

The European world, though, was permeated by suffering. The cancan delighted Mark Twain, but it was no more than the twitching of a moribund civilization. In Paris, as part of the regular tour, he visited the morgue to view the corpse of a drowned man (132). At the Château d'If, he brooded over the idea of prisoners locked away in permanent solitary confinement, especially the Man in the Iron Mask (102–4). He viewed the dungeons and torture chambers of Venice and meditated in horror on the frescoes of the Council of Three with their "pictures of death and dreadful suffering!" (224). He listened to the story of a man hanged by his chin on an iron hook and tried to exorcise it with a scoffing humor (215). He was proudly brought to see a statue of a man flayed, "every vein, muscle, every fiber and tendon of the human frame, represented in minute detail." At this dreadful sight, Twain let down his guard for a moment, saying that he regretted he had seen it, that he was certain he would dream of it, sometimes as if it were leaning over his bed and looking at him with its dead eyes, sometimes "stretched between the sheets with me and touching me with its exposed muscles and its stringy cold legs" (175). That grisly fantasy yielded in turn to an account of returning late one night when a boy and deciding to sleep in his father's office. Gradually, he realized that a form lay stretched upon the floor. It was a corpse, its eyes fixed, stabbed to death. That figure too, Mark Twain says, he has seen "often, since then—in my dreams" (177).

The progress of this particular innocent was then through halls of horror, featuring painted depictions of martyrs and statues mutilated by time; underground through tombs and catacombs, past decaying, grinning mummies; even to a dungeon in Pompeii where two charred prisoners had been burned to death in the volcanic fires. This last was a situation of peculiar vividness for Mark Twain, for he believed that as a boy he had been responsible for the death of a prisoner in the local jail, one whose cell had caught fire shortly after Twain had passed him a match to light his pipe (178, 301–2, 329; *LOM,* 290).

Which is to say that Europe revived the worst terrors of a hideous death that Mark Twain had carried in his memory from boyhood. Such feelings or something even worse may account for a curious and otherwise unexplained sentence that occurs when Twain is at Lake Como. Dramatically isolated by separate paragraphing, it is neither expanded nor otherwise explained. Here it is in its frame:

> Then to bed, with drowsy brains harassed with a mad panorama that mixes up pictures of France, of Italy, of the ship, of the ocean, of home, in grotesque and bewildering disorder. Then a melting away of familiar faces, of cities and of tossing waves, into a great calm of forgetfulness and peace.
>
> After which, the nightmare.
>
> Breakfast in the morning, and then the Lake.
>
> (201)

Aside from that undescribed nightmare, many other things were happening to this brash young traveler abroad. He began to perceive the cant of the guidebooks. The aesthetic reverence of the tourists at first amused, then irritated him. He flirted with sexual possibilities, although his fervor was quashed when he inspected the fabled *grisettes* up close, for they were ungainly, homely, had mustaches, and ate garlic (151). Similarly, the tears he and his fellows had wasted on the sentimental love story of Héloise and Abelard proved fallacious, for Abelard turned out to be no more than "a dastardly seducer" who had abused the confidences of a young girl (147).

The fraudulence of Mark Twain's guides was especially significant to him. This despicable world contained no one who could be relied on for guidance, no Vergil or Beatrice to take one safely through this inferno. The guides were in fact doubly duplicitous, because they deceived their clients to line their own pockets and because they spoke out of manifest ignorance. Twain was lost—at least there in Europe—in a stinking swamp.

All these reactions are fused in that famous mock-serious refrain that Mark Twain and his youthful co-conspirators used when the guides mechanically recounted the story of Christopher Columbus, or any of a thousand other luminaries of the European past. "Is—is he dead?" they asked (295).[2] Of course, it was a joke. But *was* all they were asked to believe in, to revere, dead? The boldness of the explorers, the eternal love stories, the glories of the Renaissance painters, the greatness of the architecture, the histories of powerful men—were these all fraudulent, or if once

2. As David Sloane points out, in Artemus Ward's "The Greenlion and Oliver Cromwell" (1867), a London landlord asks: "And this Mr. Cromwell—is he dead?" (*Mark Twain as Literary Comedian* [Baton Rouge, La., 1979], 43).

genuinely inspirational, were they now without force? Were they no more than grinning skulls in a continental catacomb? Emerson had counseled Americans to free themselves from the dead hand of the past, but a generation later a nostalgia for the fathers had revived. There was a curiosity about sources and a thirst for cultural enlargement and continuity. But once discovered, was it all to prove dead?

Given such submerged apprehensions, one is not surprised to hear Mark Twain laud Napoleon III, for even when reviled, this emperor persisted in dreaming of a crown, until at last he rather improbably gained it. Moreover, having done so, he seemed to have brought commercial prosperity to France, and security to Paris. Twain particularly admired Napoleon's having eliminated the crooked cobblestone streets into which the mob could dodge, streets they could tear up when inflamed and hurl at his majesty's troops (128, 158). Twain may seem to be offering disconcerting praise for dictatorial efficiency, but one can see that it arises out of his revulsion at a poisonous, plotting, obstreperous world. Napoleon at least meant to modernize and control it. This brought Twain to praise the French railway system, whose efficiency he attributed to the practice of hanging someone for any accident that occurred (110). The same impatient motivation obtained when Xerxes had those contractors who had built a flimsy bridge beheaded. "If our Government would rebuke some of our shoddy contractors occasionally, it might work much good," Twain remarks (357). His exasperation moved one step further toward comic exaggeration when he later declared that he wished Russia would annihilate Turkey a little, because of "the inhuman tyranny of the Ottoman Empire" (443). Underneath all the joking one can see the attraction for him of strong social measures. Still, that solution was far from satisfactory. Although Twain would repeatedly revert to the idea of the strong man who could manage the otherwise perverse human animal, he ultimately suspected that the abuses rose from deeper sources, the key to which might be found at the heart of Western spirituality.

In the *Innocents,* the pivotal point between Europe and Asia is Greece. Its cultural riches were virtually denied the party, however, since the ship had just come from Italy where a cholera epidemic was developing; the passengers, therefore, were not to land until they had remained in quarantine for eleven days. Under penalty of imprisonment if caught, Mark Twain and three others made a Tom Sawyer-ish expedition ashore at night. Although Twain was duly impressed by the Acropolis, two other eerie moments stand out in his account. Thirsty, the group picked some grapes "and were reaching down for more when a dark shape rose mysteriously up out of the shadows beside us and said 'Ho!' And so we left" (343). Although Twain would seem to be describing no more than someone pro-tecting his vines from interlopers, the description itself has an unearthly quality. The "dark shape" is not specifically human, and its exclamation is more indefinite than a warn-ing.[3] Even more disconcerting, when they reached the courtyard outside the Parthenon, where fragments of stat-ues were strewn about, "it startled us, every now and then, to see a stony white face stare suddenly up at us out of the grass with its dead eyes" (347). The dead eyes are a new de-tail, for the original notebook entry merely reads: "Grim marble faces glancing up suddenly at you out of the grass at your feet" (*N&J*1, 396).

3. Mark Twain's notebook entry is a little more informative, but not much: "We made the trip! (stopped occasionally by sav-ages armed with guns, who rose mysteriously up out of the shad-ows & darkness & said Ho! when we happened to be stealing grapes,) . . ." (*N&J*1, 389–90).

The atmosphere of Greece was not one of European corruption but of a pale, shadowed, and essentially unavailable past. When they approached the Acropolis, the party passed "a row of open graves, cut in the solid rock." Now, in the moonlight, everything seemed spectral, "alive with ghosts," while Athens below them was "like some living creature wrapped in peaceful slumber" (344, 347, 348). Twain could only catch unearthly glints of whatever the classical world might have been supposed to represent.

Coming to Mars Hill where Saint Paul had disputed with the Athenians, Mark Twain said that he had tried to recollect what the Bible said of the matter, "but for certain reasons I could not recall the words" (349). He never attempted to explain the reasons for that memory lapse but said that he had since found the biblical account, which he then quotes. It concerns Paul's reproaching the Athenians for having an altar inscribed "TO THE UNKNOWN GOD." Paul declares that he now brings that mysterious God into the light: "Whom, therefore, ye ignorantly worship, him I declare unto you" (Acts 17:23; 349). That is the end of the incident. The next paragraph begins: "It occurred to us after a while that if we wanted to get home before daylight betrayed us, we had better be moving." One cannot tell whether Twain consciously arranged this confrontation of cultures, but he highlighted the moment when it occurred, then passed on without further comment. But the idea that an unknown god, a hidden, mysterious, long-lost divinity, might finally be identified always had manifest attractions for Twain. Ironically, as he moved into the Middle East, the only God he had ever known began to lose his identity with distressing finality.

First, though, the party had to touch Turkey and Russia. What few illusions Mark Twain possessed about Turkey were swiftly dispelled. The boatmen in Constantinople were "the awkwardest, the stupidest, and the most unscien-

tific on earth" (358). The city itself was "the very heart and
home of cripples and human monsters" and "everybody"
there "lies and cheats" (361, 370). Saint Sophia's was "the
rustiest old barn in heathendom" and its floor was covered
with "a complication of gums, slime, and general corruption" (362). Nor could a Turkish bath cleanse the corruption. It was all "a malignant swindle" (380).

Had there been a Hercules to clean the Augean stables of
Constantinople, no doubt Mark Twain would have celebrated him as he did Napoleon III for bringing order to
Paris. But Twain's ambivalence about earthly figures of
power appeared when the ship moved on to Yalta. There the
party met Alexander II. Twain was taken by his physical
height, his courtesy, and his air of kindness. Most of all, he
was impressed at the tremendous autocratic power the czar
possessed over seventy million people, for all of them
would at a nod "spring to his bidding" (395). But contemplating this epitome of political power, Twain reverted
to democratic aggression. "Here was a man who could do
this wonderful thing, and yet if I chose I could knock him
down." Further, he avowed that if he could have, he would
have stolen the czar's coat—just to have "something to remember him by" (395).

As the party finally approached the Holy Land, the com-
mentary began to focus on Christianity in its early guises.
Much of Mark Twain's reaction is satiric and skeptical.
The Seven Sleepers of Ephesus, those Christian Rip Van
Winkles, were thieves from the start; and after they awoke
from their long sleep, they were profoundly distressed:
"Our homes are desolate, our friends are dead. Behold, the
jig is up—let us die" (428). That is how Twain's parodic resurrection concludes. No wonder that at the edge of the
Holy Land, he makes the gray lizard the emblem of mockery of human vanity. It is "the color of ashes; and ashes are
the symbol of hopes that have perished." When all the

temples and palaces and empires have been built and fallen, the lizard will still survive them all. "You, who stand here and moralize over me: I will crawl over *your* corpse at the last" (489).

To be sure, a good portion of Mark Twain's animus toward organized Christianity was directed against his contemporaries, the aging pilgrims, who were vandals and souvenir hunters and who broke the spirit of religious law while keeping the letter of it; against the biblical commentators and the preachers who damaged their religion through obtuseness; and against all who would kill those who truly and fearlessly preached the reality of Christ (543, 451–52, 409, 462–63). Any idealist or imaginative human was prey for their malice. Twain remarks that when the elders saw Joseph, they "were glad. They said 'Lo, here is this dreamer—let us kill him'" (493). And the "image-breakers and tomb-desecrators" of the *Quaker City* were of a piece with such hard-eyed men (493).

By contrast, to Mark Twain's mind, there had once been a superior order of beings. For him, the authors of the Bible had the supreme capacity for telling their stories in simple language and without intruding their own personalities (492). Christ himself had the gift of making the afflicted whole again with a word (475). But even in Christ's lifetime, oppressive layers of venality and stupidity smothered that freshness. In his notebook Twain burst out: "The people of this region in the Bible were just as they are now—ignorant, depraved, superstitious, dirty, lousy, thieving vagabonds" (*N&J*1, 425). And there too, starkly, he made this entry: "Christ been once—never come again" (*N&J*1, 449).

When his party passed through Shechem, a Samaritan community (now Nablus), Mark Twain concluded his remarks with what would appear to be a joke. He says that while there he purchased "a secret document" of "extraordinary interest" that he proposed to publish as soon as he had finished translating it (552). Presumably Twain meant to satirize new archaeological discoveries that were being oversold when announced to the public, but one also feels the desire that such potent secrets might become available, supposing they were translatable. In a sense, all Twain's travel reports were attempts to comprehend hidden meanings. Unfortunately, his interpretations were often so negative that he felt they could not be made available to the American audience. He told his notebook that the second coming was an illusion, but not his public.

Some of the Holy Land's illusory powers Mark Twain attributed to atmospheric effects. In reality the landscape was an ugly, dusty, rocky chaos, but under starlight or moonlight, it became a shimmering mystery (512–13). Still, "the magic of the moonlight is a vanity and a fraud and whoso putteth his trust in it shall suffer sorrow and disappointment" (524). The explanation for such pessimism was everywhere evident. The party entered the Middle East through crowds of beggars, cripples, lepers, and babes with flies clustered at their eyes, their mothers too apathetic to brush them away (464, 473). As the pilgrims moved toward the heart of the Christian mystery, things became progressively more miserable, more concentratedly appalling, and much less inspiring. Palestine was about the size of an American county (502). Jerusalem was but a village of four thousand (556). It was more than just a topographical observation for Twain to remark: "I must begin a system of reduction. . . . I have got everything in Palestine on too large a scale" (486). Everything. So upon reaching Bethlehem, he touched "with reverent finger, the actual spot where the infant Jesus lay, but I think—nothing" (601).

So far as this area of the world was concerned, Mark Twain's disillusionment was complete. He had found Jerusalem "mournful and dreary and lifeless." Everywhere he had been assailed by "lepers, cripples, the blind, and the idiotic"

(559). In the context of this depressing reality, he was obliged to visit tomb after tomb: that of Noah, Joseph, Jesus, Adam (443, 553, 560, 567). But everything remained stone dead. Adam generated parodic mourning, and at the grave of Jesus, Twain exploded in disdain. The site was "scandalized by trumpery, gewgaws, and tawdry ornamentation" (560). It was difficult, Twain said, not to get the impression that Christ had been crucified in a Catholic church (572).

This move back through time, first through the aesthetic pretensions and moral cynicism of western Europe, then into the sordid poverty of the Middle East, and finally to the fraudulence and dust of the Holy Land itself, constituted a primary revelation for Mark Twain. The force of the incessantly dreadful poverty quite overwhelmed him. Palestine was "a hopeless, dreary, heart-broken land" (606). All that remained of value was the memory of a good Savior. But he could not really accept the idea that this figure had once walked this ground or any ground accessible to him—"the gods of my understanding have been always hidden in clouds and very far away" (472).

If the first conclusion to the long journey took place at Jaffa when they returned to the ship—"the long pilgrimage was ended"—five more chapters and a "Conclusion" were yet to follow. *The Innocents Abroad* winds down through a series of endings. The tentativeness and variety of the book's gestures at closure suggest Mark Twain's own uncertain commitment. The great search back through time to the heart of Christianity had proved to be a terrible deception. Jaffa offered a farcical footnote to this loss of illusions in the encounter with the remnants of the "Adams Jaffa Colony." These were the humiliated followers of a prophet who, they now recognized, had "shamefully humbugged" them (613). Mark Twain identifies this leader by four roles that in his experience were always at best equivocal: actor, adventurer, Mormon, and missionary. At heart, Adams was a confidence man, no better in kind than those guide-book writers and Christian ministers and guides whom Mark Twain had learned to distrust. The same mocking reality that gave this false leader the name Adams designated a Moses as their savior—Moses Beach of the *New York Sun,* who charitably paid their fares back to Maine.

The second conclusion occurred when the party reached the Egyptian Sphinx. "After years of waiting, it was before me at last" (628). The Sphinx impressed Mark Twain deeply. He reads into its visage feelings that are often discovered in Jesus Christ. "The great face was so sad, so earnest, so longing, so patient. There was a dignity not of the earth in its mien, and in its countenance a benignity such as never any thing human wore" (628–29). There is no jeering here about a nose broken off, such as Twain had indulged in with European statues. Rather, he is impressed by the stoic impassivity of the Sphinx. It has contemplated the ocean of human misery for five thousand years, not judging it, not mocking it, not condemning it—"pathos dwells in these grave eyes"—but merely looking over and past history "*at* nothing—nothing but distance and vacancy" (629). In the presence of the Sphinx, Twain said that he felt something of what he supposed he would feel when he was at last standing "in the awful presence of God" (629). If so, it was a majestic but not a condemnatory deity. Although Twain could not incorporate the associations that the Sphinx generated in him into any acceptable cosmic system, here was a power he could revere—asexual, all-knowing, sympathetic but reserved, and ultimately above the tumult and confusion, knowing that finally nothing means anything, that at the farthest reach of this preternatural vision there was only "distance and vacancy" (629).[4]

4. Opinions differ, though. For Everett Emerson, the description of the Sphinx "goes on and on" and is no more than "senti-

The third ending descends into involvement and contempt again. It occurs with the party's actual arrival back
in New York harbor. One can detect Mark Twain's mood in
the last phrase of that chapter: "and the long strange cruise
was over. Amen" (642). But of course the book was still not
complete because the feelings of disappointment and vexa-
tion suggested by that "Amen" had to be purged one last
time, as they then were by Twain's reprinting the savagely
satiric article he had written for the *New York Herald* upon
their return. The article offended many of the passengers
because of Twain's unconcealed resentment at having spent
more than five months in the company of "venerable fos-
sils" (645). But when Twain says that the expedition might
better have been called "The Grand Holy Land Funeral
Procession," one can see that quite beyond the aged participants, much had died for him on this pilgrimage. Not that
he was a committed Christian before he visited the Holy
Land. In part he had joined the trip with the expectation
that it would afford materials to satirize. On the other
hand, Twain had not been altogether a disbeliever either,
and the tawdry grimness of the Holy Land had certainly
dispelled a number of illusions.

The "Conclusion" proper to the whole narrative was
written a year later. In a somewhat mellower mood, Mark
Twain first offered a tribute to his fellow passengers, then
turned to enumerate his memories of places visited. The
names of various important cities are listed with a characterization for each. Milan, Venice, and Rome all receive
extended descriptions, and there is "majestic Gibraltar glo-
rified with the rich coloring of a Spanish sunset and swimming in a sea of rainbows" (650). But as he comes to the

---

mental rhetoric" composed to please Olivia Langdon and Mrs.
Fairbanks (*The Authentic Mark Twain: A Literary Biography of
Samuel L. Clemens* [Philadelphia, 1984], 51, 54).

last paragraph, what had formerly been the climactic focus of the trip was now relegated to one among many places. Jerusalem was only "sacred." Twain ends both his recapitulation of the journey and his book with—one would never guess—Damascus. "Damascus, the 'Pearl of the East,' the pride of Syria, the fabled Garden of Eden, the home of princes and genii of the *Arabian Nights,* the oldest metropolis on earth, the one city in all the world that has kept its name and held its place and looked serenely on while the Kingdoms and Empires of four thousand years have risen to life, enjoyed their little season of pride and pomp, and then vanished and been forgotten!" (651).

This final ending has several revealing features. It is, first of all, a severely idealized version of the Damascus that Mark Twain had described earlier in the book. When he first saw the city from the mountain, he thought it an incredibly beautiful oasis in a rocky hell and noted that tradition claimed that this was where the Garden of Eden had been located. No more, though. Once Damascus was entered, "the paradise is become a very sink of pollution and uncomeliness" (456). The principal chapter on Damascus ends with Twain's reaction to a leper hospital there—"horrible!" (464).

But I think we can determine what drew Mark Twain to the later, sanitized celebration of Damascus. Jerusalem could not serve. It was too deeply discredited in his mind. On the other hand, the association of the Garden of Eden with Damascus placed it imaginatively in that context of the innocent and naturally beautiful beginning of mankind. The fantasies of the *Arabian Nights* also won Twain's heart with all the magic tricks associated with genii and the high dignity of princes. Like the Sphinx, Damascus also had the virtue of unusual endurance, of surviving the vicissitudes of the swarming human insect. And finally—it is the note on which the book closes—men's puniness, vulnerability, and mortality are underlined. The transcendent figure, whether Colonel Sherburn on the roof of his porch in *Huckleberry Finn,* or Satan in *The Mysterious Stranger,* or the Sphinx, is a figure superior to ordinary human pretensions and as such ever central in Mark Twain's imagination. He wanted permanence, solidity, thereness. This book concludes by emphasizing how much of humanity has "vanished and been forgotten."

3

A symmetry exists between *The Innocents Abroad* and *Roughing It,* inadvertent, perhaps, but nonetheless there. The first book crosses the Atlantic, travels east through European culture to the old heart of Christian spiritual life. The second travels west on a physical odyssey to a crude but vital frontier, then moves out into the Pacific to the heart of a primitive, supposedly Edenic, culture. *Roughing It* is the more comfortable book, more amused, revivified, energetic. Although aware of the shortcomings of life in the far West, Mark Twain adapted to it with a cheerful admiration. Without necessarily championing its superiority, *Roughing It* affirms the value of American life in the raw.

The relationship of the two areas had been in Mark Twain's mind during the *Quaker City* expedition when he recorded in his notebook that his party had crossed "over a horrible rocky, barren desert (like Nevada)" (*N&J*1, 423). It remained with him in 1871 when he was composing *Roughing It.* He told his sister Pamela not only that he was "writing a book like the 'Innocents' in size and style," but also that the new book had "a great pyramid" in it (*MTL* 1:176). This pyramid was constructed of mail sacks unloaded from the stagecoach in which Twain was traveling (*RI,* 51). The West had a "grim sphynx" too. She boarded the stagecoach and sat in absorbed silence, slapping mosquitoes and contemplating their crushed bodies with satisfaction until Twain opened a conversation with her. Once stirred into speech, she rained a deluge of "dislocated grammar and decomposed pronunciation" on the passengers. "The Sphynx was a Sphynx no more!" (48–49). The West also had a new Moses in the form of a stage driver of such prodigious energy that a young American, when told that Moses had led his people for forty years over "the sandy desolation," responded: *"Forty years? Only three hundred miles?* Humph! Ben Holliday would have fetched them through in thirty-six hours!" (74). Here were the first symbolic indications that *Roughing It* would take its readers in a direction opposite, thematically as well as geographically, to that followed in *The Innocents Abroad*.

The authorial attitude differs too. Although Mark Twain plays the innocent on this trip as well, he does so cheerfully. He encounters just as many frauds, obstacles, and disillusionments as he had in Europe and the Holy Land, but now they tend to strike him as amusing. Essentially, *Roughing It* dramatizes how ignorant the narrator then was, how naive; how deceptive the world was and is; and how cruel other people can be. Yet nothing much happens that is serious. The central mood of the book is optimistically comic.

Roughing It is a book of high energy, of mostly cartoon violence. A cat is blown into the sky by a blast at a quartz mine, then drops down and lands, singed and irritable but essentially unhurt (392). Later there is another blast, this time involving a human who, while preparing explosives, accidentally sets them off and is blown so high that he looks, progressively, no larger than a boy, a doll, a bee. When *he* descends sixteen minutes later, the company docks him for the time he was away from his job (490–91). People roar down mountainsides aboard avalanches, and they fly through the air on Washoe zephyrs, but it is all for amusement, a celebration of American energy as exhibited in the land and in the people (84, 156).

It is true that the background contains brutal incidents, including people being terrorized by desperadoes and a

Chinese being stoned to death, but in the main the mood is buoyant. There's a lot of speed and vigorous motion: a swift coyote, a runaway Mexican plug, a pony express rider, earthquakes. Mark Twain's delight in the untrammeled West is manifest: it's exhilarating and yet any real dangers are conjured away. For example, Twain records being in a storm on Mono Lake. The alkali content of its waters is described as deadly. "It is nearly pure lye" (244). To swim in Mono would strip the skin from one's body. But finally, really inexplicably, Twain and his companion do swim to shore safely—"things cannnot last always" (250). At another point, Twain is lost with a party in a snowstorm. They prepare to succumb. "Oblivion came. The battle of life was done" (220). Then they suddenly discover that they are but fifteen steps away from a stage station.

In each instance, Mark Twain milks the incident for melodramatic tension. On Mono Lake, he and Calvin Higbie are on an island when their boat drifts away. Will they perish? Then the boat floats back. Higbie prepares to leap into it. Will he make it? In the snowstorm, the party tries to start a fire with pistol shots, then discovers four matches. Each one is illuminated, then extinguished. It is all stimulating nonsense, carried on the crest of Twain's exuberance. *Roughing It* is a youthful book rather than a disconcerting pilgrimage in the company of sour patriarchs.

The triumph of such apparently dangerous but actually benign occasions occurs in a poem, "The Aged Pilot Man" (332). It has the identical components of the other adventures: a storm, a terrified group of people who think themselves lost, and, in Dollinger, an indomitable leader. "Fear not, but lean on Dollinger, / And he will fetch you through" (332). A tempest pounds a canal boat, the passengers cower, the crew desperately jettisons the cargo, but it is too late—they are lost! And so in despair they embrace for the last time, grieving for the wives, mothers, and children they will never see again. At the height of this pathos "the dauntless prophet," Dollinger, vows he will bring them through safely, whereupon a wonder: a farmer lays a plank between the canal boat and the shore. That was all that was needed for salvation. This solution is as anti-climactic as would be a stranger's approaching the Ancient Mariner and simply taking the albatross from his neck. Note that the pilot turns out to be useless. The storm might be real and the leader undaunted, but all his heroic posing is irrelevant. Mark Twain was throwing his comic genius behind a truth he very much wanted to believe: that simple, practical solutions exist for the worst dilemmas. People may be liable to panic, but the poem, like the conclusion to the Mono Lake episode and to the enveloping snowstorm, attests that however the world may frighten us, it is manageable.

Much later on, in the Sandwich Islands, the fallibility of another authority is discovered. Captain Cook, previously taken for a god by the natives, is wounded and cries out. "It was his death warrant. Instantly a shout went up: 'He groans!—he is not a god!'" So the islanders killed and dismembered him. The final ignominy for the debased former divinity came when his heart "was found and eaten by three children who mistook it for the heart of a dog" (458). History, then (apparently), verified Mark Twain's experience when abroad in the world: gods, whether historical, artistic, or spiritual, were likely to be fraudulent or no longer of moment and so might be dispatched or ignored. At the same time, Twain kept repeating anecdotes that attested to the capacity of ordinary mortal man to survive in a roaring world. There might in fact be dangers out there, but they could mostly be circumvented or dispelled. The few that remained uncontrollable were to be designated "visitations of God" (228, 297). As time went on, though, that category enlarged, and the dangers became as genuine as the one that ended Cook's life. The latter reaches of *Roughing It* are more disquieting.

Many other and lesser illusions had to be exposed on this trip west. The narrator, a "disciple of Cooper" and "worshiper of the Red Man," had to learn through the agency of the Goshoot Indians just how romantic his notions had been, for the Indians actually turned out to be "treacherous, filthy, and repulsive," even as later in Hawaii Twain came to believe that its people, "those 'gentle children of the sun,'" "were not the salt of the earth" (442, 146).

Fraudulence permeated the frontier, as it did the rest of the world. *Roughing It* is a book of extravagant liars: Bemis, treed by a buffalo, claims it then climbed up after him; Eckert, the Englishman, said he had a cat who ate coconut; an "old Admiral" "created history" on shipboard; Markiss was so notorious a liar that when he committed suicide, no one would believe him; and then there is Mark Twain himself (77–79, 79–81, 399, 491). But gifted as he was at invention, he still had to learn to either penetrate others' fraudulence or suffer for it. He yields to the persuasiveness of an auctioneer selling a Genuine Mexican Plug, which then proves to be a bucking devil (174). He finds flakes of gold in a stream and is confident he has made his fortune, but they turn out to be only mica. Twain draws an explicit lesson of Europe versus America, of rhetoricians versus plain speakers. "Gold in its native state is but dull, unornamental stuff . . . only low-born metals excite the admiration of the ignorant with an ostentatious glitter. However, like the rest of the world, I still go on underrating men of gold and glorifying men of mica" (197).

The same contrast obtains when the fireman Scotty Briggs goes to secure the services of a minister for his friend's funeral. Scotty speaks in vivid colloquial metaphors, whereas the minister employs the strangulated idioms of a genteel education. Mark Twain's linguistic preference is never in doubt. He placed the highest value on the slang of Nevada, calling it "the richest and the most infinitely varied and copious that had ever existed" (298). This conflict of value systems is repeated when Captain Ned Blakely discovers that his black mate has been shot to death by a notorious bully. Furious, he means to hang the culprit at once, and soon enough he does, but not until he has had to plow through the scrupulosities of the other sea captains, who protest that justice must be done. The killer must be tried. "Great Neptune, *ain't* he guilty?" cries the exasperated Captain Ned. "This beats my time. Why you all *know* he's guilty" (322).

One can see in many such instances the perpetual contest of the city, the cultivated, the "sivilized" against the country, the crude, the natural. Put "Europe" in an "American" environment and it will be bested—that is Mark Twain's message. Such confrontations were always present in his imagination, starting at the outset of his career, when the squatter outwitted the dandy. In *Roughing It,* a "town-dog" with "a good opinion of himself" tries to catch a deceptively ragged coyote until he is so thoroughly bested that he slinks back to the wagon train, humbled and ashamed (67–68). This archetypal situation of being beaten also involves innocence becoming experienced. The cat, after being blown up, is indignant at those who "take advantage of a cat that 'ain't had no experience of quartz minin'" (392).

In this anarchistic world of the West, where a man had to fend for himself and hope for the best, Mark Twain could not help admiring the dominant man, even as he had Napoleon III in *The Innocents Abroad.* In *Roughing It,* Slade, a division agent of the stage company, epitomized this figure, for he was, Twain says, "at once the most bloody, the most dangerous and the most valuable citizen" of the frontier (90). Slade might have been a vicious killer, but his "coaches went through every time!" (92). Such efficiency continued to excite Twain's admiration, as did Slade's bringing order into his district. The outlaws "respected him, admired him, feared him, obeyed him!" (93).

After working in brutally demanding jobs and even risking his life as a prospector, Mark Twain failed to achieve such power himself. Even when success beckoned, something always went wrong. His partner, Calvin Higbie, finally located a rich "blind lead." Twain's explanation of this mining term is unclear, but its specifics don't matter (254). The term means for Twain exactly what it suggests. The lead promises incredible riches, but the partners' hopes for it turn out to be blind, not because the vein itself is without ore but because the two men fail to file their claim within the requisite period of ten days. Later in San Francisco, Twain again supposedly lost a million dollars because he missed an appointment to buy into a speculative mining project (374–79).

Samuel Clemens's lifelong preoccupation with discovering something that would make him a fortune—an inheritance, a mine, a book, an invention—is familiar enough and has often been identified with the general American personality. But here I wish to place this preoccupation in the context of *Roughing It*. The character Mark Twain is adrift in this book, trying out the terms the world has presented him and looking for a fortune or, failing that, at least trying to locate a satisfactory profession. One can perceive the unfocused restlessness of Mark Twain's imagination in the comments that act as transitions from one part of the book to the next. After a variety of jobs and speculative ventures in Nevada, the chapter-opening question was inevitably, "What to do next?" (265). Even after serving some time as a reporter for the *Territorial Enterprise,* Twain again grew restive. "I wanted to see San Francisco. I wanted to go somewhere. I wanted—I did not know *what* I wanted. I had the 'spring fever' and wanted a change principally, no doubt" (356).

Henry Thoreau claimed in *Walden* that he left the pond because he had several more lives to live; he told his journal he didn't know why he left; and he actually left because Emerson had requested that Thoreau take over his household while he was away on a lecture tour. In Virginia City in late May 1864, Mark Twain became embroiled in a dispute over his responsibility for publishing the rumor that certain funds being collected for the Civil War wounded were actually being diverted to support an eastern miscegenation society. The resulting furor became sufficiently heated for dueling invitations to be issued.[1] But aside from that effective stimulus for Mark Twain's departure for San Francisco, one can feel the legitimacy of his expressing an unmotivated need to move on. His pilgrimage was far from over, so that San Francisco newspapering proved to be only an interlude. Soon "the vagabond instinct was strong upon me," and Twain sailed for the Sandwich Islands as a special correspondent for the *Sacramento Union*. He traveled to a world antithetical to the Holy Land, although it was, ironically, a world now poisoned by Christian influence.

Or rather Mark Twain came to realize that the Christians brought a mixture of innovations to the islands; consequently, when he praises the new order, one cannot be altogether certain whether he is being ironic or not. Twain was clearly revolted by the primitive violence of the old Hawaiian kings, who used a combination of physical force and superstitious fears to keep their people under control. The American presence "broke up the tyrannous influence of their chiefs" (413). Yet some of the American officials were corrupt, notably the prime minister, Charles Coffin Har-

1. The controversy is detailed in *Mark Twain of the Enterprise,* ed. Henry Nash Smith (Berkeley, 1957), 25–29.

ris—"all jaw, vanity, bombast and ignorance, a lawyer of 'shyster' calibre, a fraud by nature" (431).

In their natural state, the Hawaiians seemed to lead at least a partially idyllic life, but that demi-paradise had since been perverted by the missionaries. These Christian zealots had made the natives "permanently miserable by telling them how beautiful and how blissful a place heaven is, and how nearly impossible it is to get there" (411). Yet Mark Twain's dilemma, as he groped for livable conditions for human beings, was that in the pre-Christian days, Hawaiian women had been severely oppressed and families solved overpopulation problems by "burying some of their children alive" (428). Hence Twain had to give the missionaries credit for having "liberated woman and made her the equal of man" and for having stopped the murder of children (428).[2]

Puritanical in some respects and skeptical in others, Mark Twain said mockingly in *The Innocents Abroad* that when he had viewed the cancan at the Jardin Mabille, he had placed his hands "before my eyes for very shame. But I looked through my fingers" (99).[3] He was clearly uncertain about the acceptability of this audacious display of French female flesh yet exhilarated by the tumultuous activity involved in the display—"bobbing heads, flying arms, lightning flashes of white-stockinged calves and dainty slippers in the air" (136–37). The Pacific version of all this was the hula. About it Twain was even more circumspect, calling

2. In his notebook Mark Twain made a longer list of the positive accomplishments of the missionaries, which ranged from instituting marriage and abolishing infanticide to educating the people. See *N&J*1, 154.

3. Thomas Tenney calls attention to parallel behavior in a book that Twain knew—James Jackson Jarves, *Parisian Sights* (1852), 105—in "Mark Twain's Early Travels and the Travel Tradition in Literature," dissertation, University of Pennsylvania, 1971, 72.

the dance "lascivious" and "demoralizing," so he concen-
trated on the dancers' extraordinary ability to move in uni-
son. Later, though, he jokes readily about watching "a
bevy of nude native young ladies bathing in the sea" (462).
Here, the sexuality being less overt and programmed, he
could express his attraction to it: "I begged them to come
out, for the sea was rising" (462).

So Mark Twain found a mix of the dreadful and the
beguiling both in the Hawaiian past and in its present. If
Hawaii had horrendous insects—scorpions, centipedes, ta-
rantulas—it also had splendidly exotic fruits—pineapples,
mangoes, guavas (406, 407). As for its populace, no matter
where he looked in the world, he could locate no unargu-
ably superior people or political system. Trickery, pom-
posity, savagery were all discoverable everywhere, including Hawaii. Nor could he blame any one group exclusively
for the unsatisfactory conditions. Although he distrusted
the missionaries, he was obliged to concede that along with
bringing the doctrines of guilt and eternal punishment to
the islands, they had also brought genuine enlightenment.
Much later he would have similarly mixed feelings about
the English presence in India.

Given this education in complexity, Mark Twain invents
an episode that farcically suggests the profundity of the
disharmonies that torment human existence. Twain reports
his encounter, while visiting the island of Hawaii, with a
preacher who has been disabled by trying to interpret a
letter from Horace Greeley. The humor is built on Greeley's
execrable handwriting, which makes the text of this important letter susceptible to several different interpretations, each as problematic as the next.

The underlying situation is a common one in Mark
Twain's writings: that is, he can often be found strug-
gling to extract meaning from some bewildering language, whether it be Horace Greeley's scrawl or a telephone

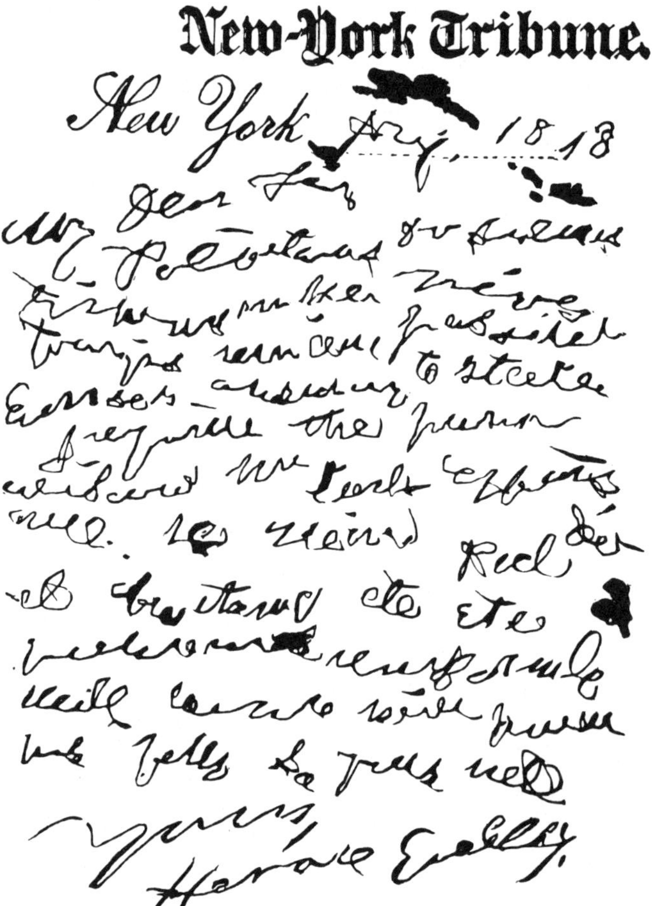

New-York Tribune.

New York, *Aug,* 1818

My dear Sir

Yours,
Horace Greeley,

conversation overheard at one end only.[4] In "trying to cipher out the meaning" of a newspaper item of some incoherence, Twain said that he was "driven to the verge of lunacy."[5] Sometimes his problem was an insufficient command of a foreign tongue. If he was not harassed and was in good spirits, the hunt for meaning became an amusing game. "There is a great and peculiar charm about reading news-scraps in a language which you are not acquainted with—the charm that always goes with the mysterious and the uncertain. You can never be absolutely sure of the meaning of anything you read in such circumstances; you are chasing an alert and gamy riddle all the time, and the baffling turns and dodges of the prey make the life of the hunt."[6]

So far as is known, Mark Twain himself created the Greeley letter. A. B. Paine reproduces a genuine Greeley holographic letter to Clemens and plausibly suggests that it served as a model for the invented version (*MTB,* 438–39). With this device, Twain found a way to liberate various surrealistic verbal associations that managed to express his moods and positions obliquely. We are not likely ever to be able to show how consciously Twain composed the five different interpretations of Greeley's hand, but no matter what degree of deliberation was involved, legitimate truths emerged. Collectively, the several readings of Greeley's letter embody precisely the enigma that Twain himself had to deal with: a scrawled world that yielded a variety of uncertain and by and large unwelcome interpretations. It's worth noting that the letter was created *after* Twain had

4. "A Telephonic Conversation," in *The $30,000 Bequest and Other Stories* (New York, 1906), 124–28.

5. "The Facts," *ET&S2,* 257.

6. "Italian Without a Master," in *The $30,000 Bequest and Other Stories,* 180.

tried to think through both his trip east to the Holy Land and his trip west through the frontier to the Pacific Islands.

The situation concerns turnips. A young man, the only son of a widow, is wholly preoccupied with turnips. They constitute the sole topic of his conversations, thoughts, and dreams. (We know, even in *Roughing It,* that the turnip is a lowly vegetable, for when Mark Twain purchases a wretched horse, one of the townsmen addresses him scornfully as "You turnip!" [174].) The young man is tormented by a fundamental problem: "He could not make of the turnip a climbing vine" (450). Hence he fell into a melancholy so profound that at last his mother asked her preacher to ask Horace Greeley what action might be taken. The task was the preacher's undoing.

The dilemma of the forlorn young man is a perpetual one: the impossibility of elevating the low and coarse into a high, civilized, and even spiritualized state of being. Mark Twain himself had observed of the Hawaiians that "superstition is ingrained in the native blood and bone," so that "the christianizing of the natives had hardly even weakened some of their barbaric superstitions, much less destroyed them" (429, 427). The problem of a determined fate was on Twain's mind and would be throughout his life. What was the likelihood of one's making any substantial improvement or even change in oneself? Nowhere that Twain had traveled had he found a class of superior beings, nor did he see in himself evidence that improvement was likely. The dilemma of the widow's son was his, then: the desire but not the capacity to transform a turnip into a climbing vine (not even through transplantation to Hartford).

The obstacles to such a transformation permeate the anecdote. *Circumstance* is the word that originally causes the preacher to recall what had driven him into a state of impotent distraction. Circumstance—the condition of being. The preacher was now sufficiently deranged to believe that the Greeley letter had caused a war in Italy; that Queen Victoria had injected herself into the controversy; and that no one had ever offered the story "straight"—"it has always been garbled in the journals" (449). For the preacher, this was the irony of the situation: a garbled message had been still further garbled in the public press, even though it affected people, including the queen, to the point of war. Eventually, the Greeley letter is correctly transcribed, but the central truth of the anecdote remains that all the evidence available to us for understanding our lives is confused, and what does come through seems to indicate that those lives are determined by both our constitution and our situation.

Still, the preacher had to learn this. Initially, he had undertaken the relief of the young man's ontological bafflement as a part of his clerical responsibilities. The obvious person from whom to ask practical advice was Horace Greeley, democrat, spokesman for self-improvement, and proponent of seeking one's fortune in the West. But on first reading Greeley's handwritten reply, the preacher had the impression that it addressed itself primarily to matters irrelevant to the case, although we can see their relation to circumstances of civilized progress, joined with fading values: "paving-stones, electricity, oysters, and something which I took to be 'absolution' or 'agrarianism,' I could not be certain which" (451). After a night's rest, the preacher reread the message. Now it seemed to say:

> Polygamy dissembles majesty; extracts redeem polarity; causes hitherto exist. Ovations pursue wisdom, or warts inherit and condemn. Boston, botany, cakes, folony undertakes, but who shall allay? We fear not. Yrxwly,

> *HEVACE EVEELOJ*

We can, I think, interpret much of this message easily enough. It has both general and specific applications.

Polygamy dissembles majesty. As we shall see, Mark Twain was preoccupied with polygamy in connection with the Mormons and more particularly with Brigham Young. In the instance of Young, taking to oneself several mates meant pretending to a condition of absolute power. Pondered more deeply, though, the capacity to entertain—to be wed simultaneously to—several creeds, although perhaps the necessary condition of modern man, still damaged the notion of omnipotence. Multiple alliances inevitably undermine central authority.

Extracts redeem polarity. One manages to balance antithetical ("polar") beliefs by selective rather than total commitments.

Causes hitherto exist. This is susceptible to two interpretations: either the forces that determine our being and behavior existed before we did, or those forces previously existed but no longer do. So either our beings are determined by preexistent causes, or this is now a meaningless universe.

Ovations pursue wisdom, or warts inherit and condemn. Either wisdom is assumed to exist and therefore praise—"ovations"—seeks it out, or we are cursed with our genetic inheritance of "warts."

Given this sobering situation, what does one do? One "undertakes" *Boston* (traditional values), *botany* (science), *cakes* (sybaritism, self-gratification), *folony* (crime or something designated crime, supposing the word to be a version of *felony*).[7] *But who shall allay?* Who shall relieve us of this condition? Not these anodynes. Nonetheless, in this first translation we have not yet succumbed. *We fear not.* In both its parts, though, the signature contains the sound of "heavy": *HEVACE EVEELOJ.*

---

7. As there is no manuscript for *Roughing It,* one cannot determine whether this is a typographical error.

The plausibility of these interpretations differs, and some phrases here and in the subsequent versions seem hardly comprehensible at all. But many of the words are easily susceptible to interpretation consonant with the underlying issues in *The Innocents Abroad* and *Roughing It.* Here, for example, is the next reading by the preacher, after he has fasted and had a night's sleep:

> Bolivia extemporizes mackerel; borax esteems polygamy; sausages wither in the east. Creation perdu, is done; for woes inherent one can damn. Buttons, buttons, corks, geology underrates but we shall allay. My beer's out. Yrxwly,
>
>

HEVACE EVEELOJ

The preacher's fasting to clear his head has obviously affected his interpretation this time. Mackerel, sausages, and beer all emerge in his consciousness. Polygamy remains in Mark Twain's mind as well. But centrally one finds a more pessimistic shorthand.

Creation perdu, is done. Our sense of having been the special, crowning creation of a divinity is lost. The world is running down; nothing is replenished. Entropy obtains. *For woes inherent one can damn.* Here is a possible response to original sin or inherited defects—one can curse God and die. Or one can try to close the gap—*buttons, buttons, corks.* Still, not only religion but also scientific discoveries are causing men to lose their stature. Man has existed less than a minute during earth's hour. Nonetheless, we shall find relief from the despair of this knowledge—*geology underrates but we shall allay.* But shall we? At least one agent of relief is no longer available: *My beer's out.*

Understandably dissatisfied with this second reading of Greeley's letter, the preacher put it aside for two days before he returned to it, "greatly refreshed" (452). He then deciphered the scrawl as follows:

Poultices do sometimes choke swine; tulips reduce
posterity; causes leather to resist. Our notions empower wisdom, her let's afford while we can. Butter
but any cakes, fill any undertaker, we'll wean him
from his filly. We feel hot. Yrxwly,
                                    HEVACE EVEELOJ

The core of this reading is a statement of despair. *Our notions empower wisdom, her let's afford while we can.* That is,
our impressions or feelings, our inclinations, our "notions"
are what actually constitute what we understand as wisdom.
Although these impressions are under attack and yielding,
still let us cling to the idea of a higher wisdom as long as we
can. But the strategy is dubious and felt to be so. *Poultices
do sometimes choke swine.* Warm, moist compresses meant to
soothe pain may in fact strangle the animal. *Butter but any
cakes, fill any undertaker, we'll wean him from his filly.* There is
some verbal echoing here—"butter but" and "fill . . .
filly"—and the meaning is not readily accessible, but an attempt to divert death appears to be involved. In any case,
we are affected by what we are slowly becoming aware
of. We are flushed, feverish, sick perhaps, perhaps even
damned. *We feel hot.*

This interpretation understandably impressed the
preacher. These "generalities" he found to be "crisp, and
vigorous, and delivered with a confidence that almost
compelled conviction; but at such a time as this, with a human life at stake, they seemed inappropriate, worldly, and
in bad taste" (452). Such a response seems natural for a
minister whose charge was to relieve the woes of his flock.
Intelligent enough to understand the implications of scientific progress, he nonetheless finds modern philosophical
speculation professionally disheartening. So he again puts
the letter aside, this time for three days, then returns to it,
with this last result:

Potations do sometimes make wines; turnips restrain
passion; causes necessary to state. Infest the poor
widow; her lord's effects will be void. But dirt, bathing, etc., etc., followed unfairly, will worm him from
his folly—so swear not. Yrxwly,
HEVACE EVEELOJ

The preacher was getting closer to the literal message;
he was genuinely making progress. But the effort was
exhausting. Since this version was just on the edge of
accuracy, its inventiveness was sacrificed to the gradual
decipherment. But we are still reminded that certain relationships obtain in the physical world. Drinking sometimes awakens the power of wine, whereas turnips hold
back passion. We do not know why, but causes must be
found and articulated. As for the troubled widow, these
mundane realities have "infested" her, rendering the truth
of her lord—God—ineffective, "void."

In desperation, the preacher finally decides to write
Greeley a second letter, this time requesting clarification. In
it he points out that although Greeley has said "causes necessary to state," in fact he has "omitted to state them"
(454). He also denies indignantly that he has "infested" the
widow or anyone else. Most pointed is his assertion that
the widow has no lord, for "he is dead—or pretended to be
when they buried him" (454). There Mark Twain provides
a succinct summary of nineteenth-century attitudes toward
the authenticity of the Resurrection.

Greeley responds with a legible copy of his letter:

Potatoes do sometimes make vines; turnips remain
passive; causes unnecessary to state. Inform the poor
widow her lad's efforts will be in vain. But diet,
bathing, etc. etc., followed uniformly, will wean him
from his folly—so fear not.
Yours,

When accurately transcribed, Greeley's message turns out to be evasively platitudinous. The young man's serious obsession is to be treated with an unspecified diet and bathing as well as with the doubly shrouded additional treatment "etc. etc." The world is as it is—potatoes sometimes transcend themselves but turnips never do—for reasons unnecessary to state. Greeley's answer is plain and simple humbug.

The minister's interpretations of Greeley's fatuous message, however, intimate the various unsettling challenges that an intelligent man of the nineteenth century, concerned with human existence, the world, and the existence of God, might face. And the Greeley letter, coupled with the unsolvable human problems obliquely referred to, effectively puts the preacher permanently out of commission. The last we hear of him, he has lapsed again "into nodding, mumbling, and abstraction" (455).

If the preacher actually existed (there is no evidence in the notebooks or original newspaper letters that anyone like him did), Hawaii had not managed to cure him of his desolation. The same was true of Mark Twain. He liked the islands' temperate climate and lazy, sensuous life, but he was revolted by the barbarities that accompanied them. The last two sights that he dwells on at some length embody his mixed feelings. On the island of Hawaii he went on horseback to "the great volcano of Kilauea" (472). The crater aroused his enthusiasm, as fires usually did. A portion of the floor of the crater "was ringed and streaked and striped with a thousand branching streams of liquid and gorgeously brilliant fire!" (474). Here was the lair of a pagan god, boiling with color and tremendously exciting, unlike the various sacred sites in the Holy Land. Everywhere were "gorgeous sprays of lava-gouts and gem-spangles" (479). It was primeval, crudely powerful, and exhilarating.

After this vitalizing experience, Mark Twain moved on to Maui, there to visit its "chief pride," the "dead volcano

of Haleakala" (484).[8] Its "yawning dead crater" proved to
be an equally extraordinary spectacle, with clouds gradually drifting into it like "a ghostly procession of wan-
derers" until the crater was filled "to the brim with a fleecy
fog." Here was the place the islanders designated "the house
of the sun" (484). But the fire had disappeared, along with its
warmth. The great primordial center of life seemed extinguished. Mark Twain, pilgrim in the throne room of primitive divinity, found himself struck dumb. "I felt like the
Last Man, neglected of the judgment, and left pinnacled in
mid-heaven, a forgotten relic of a vanished world" (486).[9]
Although that desolation was relieved shortly by the sun's
rising and casting its rich colors across the "cloud-waste,"
to Twain this display seemed "a wasteful splendor," for he
had glimpsed the white emptiness at the heart of the house
of the sun. It was as disturbing as the hot barrenness of the

8. In the original letters prepared for the *Sacramento Union,*
Mark Twain wrote only of the live volcano, Kilauea, the description of its fiery display constituting the final letter, no. 25. See
Mark Twain's Letters from Hawaii, ed. A. Grove Day (London,
1967), 291–98. Interestingly, Twain's actual itinerary led him first
to Haleakala, the dead volcano on Maui, but when after the trip
to the Holy Land he expanded his materials for *Roughing It,*
he placed the dead volcano *after* the live one, at the end of the
book. Even while he was in the islands, though, the idea of extinguished power was in his mind, for he entered in his notebook:
"Brown called his horse Haleakala—extinct volcano—because if
ever been any fire in him all gone out before *he* came across him"
(*N&J*1, 119).

9. In his first lecture, the description of his feelings was somewhat different, but equally dismal: "A feeling of loneliness comes
over a man which suggests to his mind the last man at the flood,
perched high upon the last rock, with nothing visible on any side
but a mournful waste of waters, and the ark departing dimly
through the distant mists and leaving him to storm and night and
solitude and death!" (*MTB,* 1603).

Holy Land. Neither end of the world, then, held out true hope. The heart of both the dominant Christian religion and that of the natives of paradise was hollow and dead. Not that Mark Twain had yet reached that state of arid pessimism into which Melville fell in the 1850s. He could still refer, without irony, to the dawn as "the coming resurrection" (486). Still, the last Hawaiian chapter in *Roughing It,* which immediately succeeds the trip to the dead volcano, significantly concerns a liar of monumental gifts (487–91).

In his narrative Mark Twain returned himself regretfully to San Francisco and an uncertain future. As with the *Innocents,* he experienced considerable difficulty in bringing *Roughing It* to a close. It winds down through two chapters, a "Moral," and three appendices. Twain tells first of his premier lecture. He had been so anxious about it that he had placed friends in the audience to laugh on cue. Despite his anxieties, the lecture was a great success, save for one, self-created, disappointment when he "delivered a bit of serious matter" (495). He had been particularly fond of this moment; nonetheless, after he spoke, with an inexplicable perversity, he smiled at the wife of a friend, who, given that cue, laughed, setting off the whole audience. "My poor little morsel of pathos was ruined" (496).[10]

This was a familiar situation for Mark Twain. Like most humorists, he was essentially a pensive man, and it often rankled him that people expected a joke from him rather than thoughtful observations or, as in this instance, that people mistook his seriousness for humor. But as was ex-

10. Paul Fatout finds no evidence in contemporary reviews that such a moment took place. Moreover, he likens the story to "an almost identical plot" prepared for the first night of Goldsmith's *She Stoops to Conquer* (*Mark Twain on the Lecture Circuit* [Bloomington, Ind., 1960], 39–40).

plicitly the case here, Twain himself was often responsible for diverting his audience from his gravity, and that, I think, was the essential point of this otherwise labored and inappropriate story—"in spite of all that I could do I smiled" (496).

The last formal chapter of *Roughing It* reverses this situation. Instead of a serious moment being turned into a joke, a practical joke turns out to have serious consequences. One night after lecturing in Gold Hill, Mark Twain hiked up the hill in order to descend on the other side into Virginia City. At the "divide," or crest, of the hill he was accosted by bandits going under the names of Southern Civil War generals. The robbery, however, turned out to be a hoax. The bandits were friends and still other acquaintances were hidden off the road, observing the prank. This Nevada Gadshill provided two more surprises. First, the men had waited so long for Twain "on the cold hill-top" that they were thoroughly chilled, so the tables were turned on them—except that Twain himself also caught "a cold which developed itself into a troublesome disease and kept my hands idle some three months, besides costing me quite a sum in doctor's bills" (501).

Not much of this is funny or informative. The best one can say for the protracted episode is that it involves matters of more than normal significance for Twain: that is, the assumption of false identities, especially those parodying the Confederate military leadership, went to the core of his reason for being in the Nevada Territory in the first place. To hear along with Twain the imposter's whispers—"Beauregard, hide behind that boulder; Phil Sheridan, you hide behind that other one; Stonewall Jackson, put yourself behind that sage-brush there"—is to experience the same diminution of authority that Twain concocted at the Whittier birthday dinner when he imagined frontier ruffians having taken on the identities of Longfellow, Emerson, and Oliver Wendell Holmes (500; the Whittier speech is in *MTB*, 1643–47).[11]

The Civil War represented a complex question of loyalties for someone like Mark Twain from a border state. As late as 1901 in a speech on Lincoln's birthday, he said of the war: "We of the South were not ashamed; for, like the men of the North, we were fighting for flags we loved" (*MTSp*, 230).[12] Clemens, of course, had experienced only a brief career in Missouri with "the Marion Rangers" before he decamped for the Nevada Territory.[13] His friend Joseph T. Goodman, the editor of the *Territorial Enterprise,* recalled that at the outset of the Civil War, the Nevada Territory "had proportionately a greater number of Southerners and sympathizers with the South than any other part of the Coast." According to Goodman, however, news of the battle of Bull Run made the Unionists assert themselves, so that henceforth little opposition to the war was openly heard in Virginia City.[14] Still, Twain did eventually offend the town's gentry with his imputations that the funds col-

11. Since Phil Sheridan was a well-known *Union* general in the cavalry, his name is a problem here. Because Twain refers to "their rebel brother-generals of the South," it would appear to have been mistakenly used (499). If so, though, it was an odd mistake for Twain to make and for his readers to miss. One *could* interpret Twain's reference as suggesting that the leaders of both sides of the Civil War victimized the average American, but the grounds for doing so with any confidence seem insufficient.

12. A variant of this line appears in *Mark Twain Speaking,* ed. Paul Fatout (Iowa City, Iowa, 1976), 382.

13. "The Private History of a Campaign That Failed," in *The American Claimant and Other Stories and Sketches* (New York, 1899), 237.

14. Joseph T. Goodman, *Heroes, Badmen, and Honest Miners,* intro. Phillip I. Earl (Reno, Nev., 1977), 39, 41–42.

lected for the hospitals were going to support a miscegenation society. And in 1867 James W. Nye, governor of the Nevada Territory, failed to appear to introduce Mark Twain at a New York lecture; he later explained: "I never intended to show up. . . . He's nothing but a damned Secessionist" (*MTBus,* 93). Although the subject awaits deeper analysis, we can say that the issue of the Confederacy aroused ambiguous emotions in Mark Twain, such as may account for his including the robbery-hoax by "Confederate generals" in *Roughing It.* Beyond that, though, the episode only adds rueful evidence of the volatility of humor. In fact, Mark Twain said that the experience had caused him to give up the practical joke forever.

Small wonder. As he was composing *Roughing It,* circumstances were making him the butt of the most serious mockery. His wife's father died. A woman friend of Livy's contracted typhoid fever and died in the Clemenses' house. Livy herself collapsed from the strain of nursing her friend, and a little over a month later she was delivered prematurely of their first son. Mark Twain felt distinctly oppressed: "I have been trying to write a funny book, with dead people and sickness everywhere" (*MTB,* 435). Whatever his vicissitudes may have been while he lived in the West, he said farewell to the frontier in *Roughing It* with undisguised nostalgia. It was "the friendliest land and livest, heartiest community on our continent" (501). But that tribute is immediately followed by successive miseries. Cholera broke out on the steamer he took to New York, and "home" (Hannibal), where he subsequently went to visit and to lecture, seemed dreary to him. Children were growing up and few of the adults "remained . . . prosperous and happy." The rest, he said, had left, or were in jail, or had been hanged. The identical experience would recur during the 1882 Hannibal visit recounted in *Life on the Mississippi.* Was it intended to be humorous in *Roughing It?*

Given the cumulative exaggerations of the sentence, it might be but does not seem so. "These changes," he goes on, "touched me deeply." So he joined the *Quaker City* expedition "and carried my tears to foreign lands" (502). Even if implicitly mocked, chagrin is close to the surface here.

At this point, an uncertain "Moral" concludes the main body of *Roughing It*. Mark Twain was always given to satirizing morally instructive literature, and that inclination seems to have suggested his supplying a last admonition. It proposes that if you are "of any account, stay at home and make your way by faithful diligence." If like Twain in his early young manhood, however, you are judged to be of "no account," then leave home so that "you will *have* to work, whether you want to or not. Thus you become a blessing to your friends by ceasing to be a nuisance to them—if the people you go among suffer by the operation" (502).

That final clause is something of a problem. Does it mean that you will please your old friends not only when you relieve them of the spectacle of your shiftlessness but also when they realize that you are now imposing that spectacle on others? That is, is a degree of *Schadenfreude* being posited here? Or is the meaning merely that your friends at home will be happy to have you gone, *even though* the new people among whom you will work must "suffer" your presence? Obscure as the sentence is made by its phrasing, Twain undoubtedly had his own experience in mind. He had written his mother in 1863 that he was "naturally a lazy, idle good-for-nothing vagabond," and so "I don't suppose I shall ever be any account." At the time, however, his condition pleased him. "I fare like a prince wherever I go . . . and I am proud to say that I am the most conceited ass in the Territory" (*MTL* 2:92). In *Roughing It,* though, the mood of the "Moral" is more ironically subdued.

Coupled with his preceding account of the cholera outbreak, of old friends in jail and hanged, and of carrying his
tears to foreign lands, it is a curiously unsettling and negative ending to a fundamentally high-spirited book.

Except that it has not yet ended. Like the *Innocents,
Roughing It* jolts down through a number of atmospheric
layers before it finally lands. In fact, in popular editions the
Sandwich Islands material is sometimes omitted as not ger-
mane to a narrative concerned with the colorful old West.
But even after the islands interlude comes the account of
the first lecture, the fake robbery, and the "Moral" and
then three appendices, amounting to about thirty pages
in all.

The first two appendices concern the Mormons. Mark
Twain had already described Salt Lake City's Mormon es-
tablishment and its leader, Brigham Young. His reactions
to them were decidedly mixed. The Mormons were people
of account who collectively constituted a golden beehive of
admirable industry and probity (115). At the same time,
they indulged in various practices that Twain regarded as
dubious, ranging from having a monopoly on their own
locally produced drink, "valley tan," to breaking a contract
with a non-Mormon constructing a telegraph line, to prac-
ticing polygamy, to publishing a bible that was "chloro-
form in print," to using their death squads, the "Destroy-
ing Angels," to murder obstreperous "Gentiles" (115–27).

The first appendix is essentially sympathetic toward the
Mormons for having endured persecution until they reached
their promised land, which they then improved. Mark
Twain was normally the friend of the harassed, although
paradoxically, as we have seen, he also admired powerful
men like Napoleon III and the desperado Slade. Here it was
Brigham Young who played the role of a man of "superior
brain and nerve and will" who established himself as "absolute monarch" through a combination of gall, force, and

guile (504, 507). Twain realized Young's shortcomings but could not resist his dominant personality. This awe of authority is translated in the book proper into that comic moment when during an interview with "the King," Young glances at Twain like "a benignant old cat," then puts his hand on the writer's head and inquires of Orion Clemens, "Ah—your child, I presume? Boy, or girl?" (117). This devastating question very well renders what it must have felt like to be a psychological child in the presence of that elemental force.

The second appendix counteracts the sympathy extended in the first. It deals with the atrocious "Mountain Meadows Massacre." The Mormons, disguised as Indians, attacked an emigrant train; then when their siege had failed, they proposed a truce. When the emigrants accepted the proposal, the Mormons forthwith butchered a hundred and twenty defenseless people. Mark Twain delivers this account with virtually no commentary, for the facts themselves adequately attest to the treachery and viciousness. Because these appendices were missing from the authorized English edition of *Roughing It,* Franklin Rogers has proposed that they were added "to increase the book beyond the length represented by the prospectus" (*RI,* 21). However that may be, the two antithetical appendices do manage to convey Twain's ambiguous feelings about the Mormons, which he could not otherwise synthesize into a single characterization.

The last appendix, "Concerning a Frightful Assassination That Was Never Consummated," is by far the most enigmatic. The account is long but essentially simple. It revolves around one Conrad Wiegand, a radical newspaperman and gold assayer living in Gold Hill, Nevada. After publishing charges in his newspaper, the *People's Tribune,* against several important people in Nevada mining for their exploitation of the miners, Wiegand first lost much of his assaying business; then was threatened and attacked in the street; and finally was lured into an underground office where after he refused either to name the author of the offensive article or to retract it, one of the accused repeatedly struck him with a rawhide whip.

Now whereas the Mormon materials are extensions of the Salt Lake City chapters in the main body of the book, the Conrad Wiegand appendix is attached to nothing in particular. The incidents took place early in 1870, long after Mark Twain had left Nevada. They involve no one previously mentioned in the text, and one can say of the situation only that in the book proper Mark Twain had never explored the issue of miner exploitation, even though he had declared how common corruption was in mining speculation and "how hard and long and dismal a task it is to burrow down into the bowels of the earth and get out the coveted ore" (233). One might then have expected sympathy for the miners, but it was not forthcoming.

Mark Twain's attitude can perhaps be explained by the identity of Wiegand's assailant, John B. Winters, president of the Yellow Jacket Silver Mining Company, an old friend whom Clemens had praised in the columns of the *San Francisco Call*.[15] Still, during a trip back to Nevada in 1868, Twain had been presented with a bar of silver bullion by Wiegand, wittily inscribed: "Mark Twain—Matthew V: 41—Pilgrim." The biblical citation reads: "And whosoever shall compel thee to go a mile, go with him twain."[16] But

15. See *Clemens of the "Call,"* ed. Edgar M. Branch (Berkeley, 1969), 306, n. 107. On the other hand, Clemens also attacked corrupt mining company officials in the *Call*. See pp. 238–42. This John B. Winters, by the way, should not be confused with John D. Winters, who was in the Nevada Territory at the same time and was known to Clemens. See *ET&S*1, 339.

16. Effie Mona Mack, *Mark Twain in Nevada* (New York, 1977), 355.

that failed to diminish Twain's negativity. Twain offers Wiegand's story as it was printed in the *Territorial Enterprise* but precedes it with a condescending introduction and then intersperses Wiegand's narrative with bracketed satiric commentary. By the time the fifteen pages devoted to the incident are over, Twain has worked himself into a fury. Whereas he starts by designating Wiegand "a harmless man," "an oyster that fancied itself a whale," by the end he is saying that the whipping was a "merited castigation" and that Wiegand deserved "to be thrashed" (515, 530).

Wiegand certainly was peculiar—he suspected that he had managed to keep his assailant from murdering him only by literally mesmerizing him—but he was also clearly a brave and prudent man, devoted to democratic rights, to journalistic confidentiality of sources, and to a free press. Although at the time he was writing *Roughing It* Mark Twain was part owner and editor of the *Buffalo Express,* he showed no sensitivity whatsoever to such issues. As a matter of fact, in 1873, a year after *Roughing It* appeared, he gave a speech in which he inveighed against "the license of the press," which, he said, "has scorched every individual of us in our time" (*MTSp,* 50). Nor did he display any sympathy for Wiegand's conviction that sooner or later he would be assassinated, "though it may take years to compass it" (530). Rather, Twain's indignation was directed against views that he regarded as slanderous.

This in itself is odd because when Wiegand was being threatened, he pointed out to his enraged attacker that the offensive article had said of the charges: "*Such an investigation MIGHT* result in showing some of the following points." Then followed eleven specifications, and the succeeding paragraph concluded that the proposed investigation "might EXONERATE those who are generally believed guilty" (522–23). That argument convinced Mark

Twain no more than it did the accused: "When a journalist maligns a citizen, or attacks his good name on hearsay evidence, he deserves to be thrashed for it, even if he *is* a 'noncombatant' weakling" (530). Twain would concede only that the confrontation should have taken place not in a hidden cellar but on the public street.

No commentator on *Roughing It* has ever mentioned the Conrad Wiegand appendix, because, I suppose, its presence is internally inexplicable. With his usual common-sense acuity, Edmund Wilson did ask in his journal: "And what is the reason for the last of the Appendices? The unfortunate journalist, 'half-witted' though he may have been, obviously behaved very well in standing up to those two men, one of whom had threatened to kill him (and M. T. has told you in no uncertain terms that killing was easy and frequent), and refusing to sign a retraction. Why does M. T. hold him up to ridicule, jeering at him between paragraphs?"[17]

Mark Twain himself justified including the Wiegand story by a hyperbolic claim: "It is the richest specimen of journalistic literature the history of America can furnish, perhaps" (516). The account is nothing like that, however. If it possesses any significance, it must be a personal one for Twain, one derived from feelings accumulated during his two pilgrimages. Thematically, *Roughing It* really ends in the crater of that dead volcano on Maui. At that point we can see the terminus of two contrary trips: one to the fount of Christianity, the other to mid-Pacific hedonism. And not in the supposedly sophisticated world of Europe, or in the supposedly sacred Middle East, or on the vigorous frontier, or in the pagan tropics had Mark Twain been able

17. Edmund Wilson, *The Forties,* ed. Leon Edel (New York, 1983), 279.

to find a culture he thought worthy of emulation. All was mixed, wracked with contradictions, perhaps even cursed. Corruption prevailed. To this unsettling perception of universal deception and antagonism, one possible response was that Conrad Wiegand should have known better than to attack things as they were. The strong will prosper. The rest will be thrashed.

4

With satisfactory conditions for existence unavailable at opposite ends of the earth, Mark Twain sought them in his
youth—and found them too, although again he demonstrated that they were unavailable to him personally. "Old
Times on the Mississippi," which describes his youthful
apprenticeship as a pilot, originally appeared as a series of
seven articles in the *Atlantic*. Before the rest of the book
was undertaken, Mark Twain had completed *Tom Sawyer*
and *A Tramp Abroad*. For that reason, I would like to discuss the final product, *Life on the Mississippi,* as two discrete
works, with a space of seven or eight years between their
separate creations.

"Old Times on the Mississippi" is a lively, energetic account of an unconcluded apprenticeship. It renders the
world from the perspective of a youth attracted to an adult
world of excitement and power. At the outset, Mark Twain
offers one of his charming bravura descriptions, here of
how the arrival of a steamboat would briefly animate a le-
thargic Southern town drowsing in the summer heat (28–
29). The ambitious young men inevitably wanted access to
the steamboat and the respect it commanded. There might
be humbugs and imposters in this riverboat society, but it
was preeminently the domain of authentic capability. Twain
presents the pilot as monarch of the river kingdom, "the
only unfettered and entirely independent human being that
lived in the earth" (90). Physically elevated above everyone
else on the boat and possessing absolute power while in

command, the pilot was one version of Twain's transcendent figure.[1] Even from his present perspective of apparently rising literary success, Twain still retrospectively envied the pilot of his imagination, for "writers of all kinds are manacled servants of the public. We write frankly and fearlessly, but then we 'modify' before we print" (90).

Mark Twain had attempted to enter this aristocratic river world because the pilots in charge seemed to him demigods, serenely masterful, effortlessly in control. One, Horace Bixby, agreed to instruct Twain in the mysteries, but the professional secrets of piloting proved daunting, and the demands on Twain's memory, sensibility, and confidence overwhelmed him. His superb account of the ever-expanding range of knowledge he had to absorb can, by analogy, stand for the awe any apprentice feels when first facing the apparently limitless field of his profession. But in Twain's case there is never any unequivocal triumph of achievement. He offers no account of a day when he took command and came through. Rather, the description of his education in "Old Times" chronicles a series of frustrations and humiliating defeats that were at least psychically true, and, as it happens, prophetic.

He first had to face the extraordinary complexity of the subject he was undertaking to learn—that is, the channel of the Mississippi River from St. Louis to New Orleans. Then he realized that his acquired knowledge still suffered four-hour gaps in it, caused by his time off watch. Worse, once learned by day, the river had to be relearned by night when all was changed. And when that was managed, he discovered that as the river rose or fell, its contours changed yet again. Although told with comic rue, Twain's account never

1. Paul Baender created this useful term in his dissertation, "Mark Twain's Transcendent Figure," University of California, 1956.

displays any developing mastery; rather, new, seemingly impossible, demands continue to be piled on his anxious sensibility.

In Mark Twain's account, cool pilots slipped effortlessly through fearsome shoals where the slightest error in judgment would "destroy a quarter of a million dollars' worth of steamboat and cargo in five minutes, and maybe a hundred and fifty human lives into the bargain" (51). Given this tremendous responsibility, it was no wonder that Twain's nerve repeatedly failed. He could not learn to trust what he knew and to act on it. The typical scene in "Old Times" is that of the cub, Mark Twain, at the wheel with his mentor Bixby concealed somewhere. Then, confronted with an emergency, Twain would fail, invariably setting off the indignant rage of Bixby and the hilarity of the onlookers.

Mark Twain invested considerable imaginative energy in this sequence of humiliating failure. The myth was at once satisfying and crippling for him. The existence of competent pilots steering masterfully through the shifting dangers of existence assured Twain that such control was possible, that if one were the right person, one could dominate the frightening chaotic rush of industrializing America. There was a key to such control, could one only grasp it. In his active life Twain worked furiously to do so, meeting deadlines, whipping on recalcitrant and dim editors, fighting off publishing pirates, and always affirming the superiority of that youthful river world. "I am a person who would quit authorizing in a minute to go to piloting," he wrote Howells while composing "Old Times," "if the madam would stand it." Then, however, his jokey imagination made the revealing turn: "I would rather sink a steamboat than eat, any time" (*MTHL* 1:50). He always remembered his failures. The created memories of "Old Times" embody his conscious frustration with his inability to master a glory-laden adult world. "I was a cipher in this august company," he remembered (47). There was too much to learn, what had to be learned shifted its identity with disconcerting rapidity, and what he thought he saw was not necessarily what he supposed it to be.

The famous "pilot and passenger" reactions to the river in chapter 9, "Continued Perplexities," show how the beauty and poetry that a passenger sees are drained out of a landscape when they are interpreted by the professional. The pilot knows that "this sun means that we are going to have wind to-morrow" and that that "long ruffled trail that shone like silver" is really caused by a hidden snag (63). The aesthetically compelling detail turns out to be deadly. But there was worse. The opposite was true as well. After panicking in the pilothouse trying to avoid what he took to be a "bluff reef," Twain is ordered to steer straight for it. "I held my breath; but we slid over it like oil." Bixby explains that it was but a "*wind* reef." Twain responds: "But it is exactly like a bluff reef. How am I ever going to tell them apart?" Bixby's answer: "I can't tell you. It is an instinct. By and by you will just naturally *know* one thing from the other, but you never will be able to explain why or how you know them apart" (61–62).

Although Mark Twain comments that Bixby's words "turned out to be true," his dramatized experience denies it (62). In "Old Times" he never learns to trust his knowledge, to act on what he knows rather than on what he seems to see. With a knowledge of the river in mind, one must, Bixby says, steer straight into apparent disaster without flinching. "You boldly drive your boat right into what seems to be a solid, straight wall (you knowing very well that in reality there is a curve there), and that wall falls back and makes way for you" (53). But Twain's anticipation of disaster was too powerful and repeatedly paralyzed him.

Most significant is the last episode involving Mark Twain as a cub. After that, he merely offers a few disconnected anecdotes about other men on the river and an account of the pilots' union. The culminating humiliation takes place one day when Bixby has left Twain at the wheel. After instilling in him a seed of doubt about an upcoming crossing, Bixby retires while an audience of "fifteen or twenty people" gathers. Suddenly, Mark Twain is struck by a "wave of coward agony" (88). He imagines he sees a shoal ahead in waters where a moment earlier he had proclaimed he couldn't touch bottom with a church steeple. Meanwhile the captain and mate have ordered the leadsman to begin calling out the bottom depth. The cries come: "D-e-ep four!" "The terror of it took my breath away." Then, "M-a-r-k three! M-a-r-k three! Quarter-less-three! Half twain! This was frightful!" Finally: "Quarter twain! Quarter twain! *Mark* twain!" At the italicized cry of his pen name: "I was helpless" (99).

There is no doubting the intentionality of either the emphasis or the conjunction of danger and his name. The announcement of "*Mark* twain!" paralyzes him. It signals disaster so close that for the moment he is stunned. In another moment, as the leadsman announces the progressive fragmentation of "twain"—"quarter-less-twain!"—he is led to implore the engineer below to reverse engines. At this point Bixby emerges to reveal the trick played on him, while the observers burst into "a thundergust of humiliating laughter" (89). Twain had again failed to have confidence in the certain knowledge that he possessed, and it had shattered his identity.

To be sure, at the time of this very likely invented incident, he was not yet "Mark Twain." The significance of that name only emerges for the reader aware of Twain's subsequent literary success. Then all the potentiality for irony comes to bear upon the warning. That Twain's position as a writer was profoundly insecure as well as, in some respects, unwelcome could hardly be spelled out in "Old Times," although it could not be more clearly dramatized than with the paralyzing cry of "*Mark* twain!" Related quotations illuminatingly bracket this passage from "Old Times" composed in the middle seventies. Writing to his brother Orion in 1871, Twain exclaimed in exasperation: "Haven't I risked cheapening myself sufficiently by a year's periodical dancing before the public but must continue it? I lay awake all last night aggravating myself with this prospect of seeing my hated *nom de plume* (for I do loathe the very sight of it) in print *again* every month" (*MTLP,* 57). Then at the end of 1877, on the occasion of the Whittier birthday dinner speech, Twain recalled a miner who had been put upon by three men posing as writers. Twain revealed their fraudulence to the miner, who "investigated me with a calm eye for a while; then said he, 'Ah! imposters, were they? Are you?'" (*MTB,* 1647).

The profundity of Mark Twain's ambivalence about his identity as a writer as well as his pervasive underlying insecurities as a man are familiar enough topics, but never more dramatically illustrated than at this moment when the calling out of his pen name brought terror, succeeded by humiliation.

The concluding part of "Old Times" reaffirms not only the superiority of the rank of pilot—"a king without a keeper, an absolute monarch who was absolute in sober truth"—and Mark Twain's devotion to that calling—"I loved the profession far better than any I have followed since"—but also the present inaccessibility of piloting as a profession because steamboating had been destroyed by a combination of the Civil War, the railroads, and a new method of transporting goods involving tugboats towing barges on the river: "Behold, in the twinkling of an eye, as it were, the association and the noble science of piloting were things of the dead and pathetic past!" (90, 91, 105).

This permanently closes off piloting as it once was. The

golden days had passed. Although the public "knows" that Mark Twain did eventually become a pilot and presumably partook of the eminence of that role, *Life on the Mississippi* hardly acknowledges that success. When "Old Times" was incorporated into the larger *Life,* Twain had to provide a transition to his account of the retrospective trip he took down the river twenty-one years later. One chapter of this connective material, "A Catastrophe," tells of the lingering death of Clemens's brother Henry from injuries he suffered when the boilers of the steamboat *Pennsylvania* exploded. The last sentence of the chapter reads: "His hour had struck; we bore him to the death-room, poor boy" (133). The following chapter, "A Section in My Biography," begins: "In due course I got my license. I was a pilot now, full-fledged" (134). The conjunction of the painful death of his brother and this laconic announcement is incongruous, unless, as I think is the case, the general feeling that invested Twain's becoming a pilot remained one of ambivalence and even negativity. Certainly the energetic comedy with which Twain rendered his failures as a cub has disappeared. The flatness here runs precisely contrary to the sense of exuberance and confidence one might expect as a result of his finally mastering this most desirable of occupations. Listen to this·first paragraph. It is all we are ever given about Twain's days as a certified pilot:

> In due course I got my license. I was a pilot now, full-fledged. I dropped into casual employments; no misfortunes resulting, intermittent work gave place to steady and protracted engagements. Time drifted smoothly and prosperously on, and I supposed—and hoped—that I was going to follow the river the rest of my days, and die at the wheel when my mission was ended. But by and by the war came, commerce was suspended, my occupation was gone.
>
> (134)

This is not the occasion for a careful consideration of the
evidence bearing upon Mark Twain's piloting career. It is a
topic swarming with questions. But putting aside the historical evidence, we can still see that the writing itself offers
internal puzzles. Why immediately following an account of
his brother's death should Twain move to a summary of his
history as a pilot? (Incidentally, Clemens believed that he
had killed Henry by accidentally administering an exces-
sive dose of morphine to relieve his suffering [*MTB,* 142–
43].) Why should Twain not offer a range of knowledgable
and humorous ancedotes about his new life as a pilot? And
why should he give up this most prestigious of professions
to explore with his brother the dubious potentialities of the
Nevada frontier?[2]

Mark Twain provides an ostensible answer: "The war
came, commerce was suspended, my occupation was gone"
(134). But this was not strictly true. A. B. Paine tells us
"there was a pressing war demand for Mississippi pilots"
(*MTB,* 163). Moreover, the eventual chief of the Union
River Service was none other than Horace Bixby, who not
only had trained Twain but had become a full partner with
him upon Twain's completion of his apprenticeship (*MTB,*
161, 145). It is true that Twain elected to associate himself
with the Confederacy, but as "The Private History of a
Campaign that Failed" tells us, he quickly withdrew from
the cause. It may be that political loyalties were the deciding
factor in Twain's decision to leave the river, but the prepon-
derance of evidence in "Old Times" suggests that it was

2. The most recent and authoritative consideration of the evidence is Edgar M. Branch, "Mark Twain: The Pilot and the
Writer," *Mark Twain Journal* 23, no. 2 (Fall 1985): 28–43. Branch
concludes that in his actual piloting career as opposed to its imaginative reconstruction, Clemens "was neither timid and fearful nor
incompetent, but cautious and able" (31).

rather the strain of facing the hazards of the river that made him relinquish that position. He was emphatic about his decision in an August 1862 letter to his sister: "I never have *once* thought of returning home to go on the river again, and I never expect to do any more piloting at any price" (*MTL* 1:85).

Imaginatively speaking, Mark Twain's immersion in the memories of his cubdom on the river did generate a whole new, deeper, level of reminiscence involving Hannibal, so that shortly he began to work on *Tom Sawyer* and then on *Huckleberry Finn,* before finally arranging in 1882 the trip down the Mississippi that would result in the full *Life.* But another travel book intervened, the mood of which must be considered first. Before the somberness of *Life on the Mississippi,* some exuberance was still available for display in *A Tramp Abroad.*

5

Much of *A Tramp Abroad* is based on a walking tour that Mark Twain made in the summer of 1878 through the Black Forest and Alps with his friend Joe Twichell.[1] He regarded the trip as "a rich holiday," but its transformation into a marketable product proved less restful (*MTL* 1:338). Writing Howells early in its composition, he observed that "a man can't write successful satire except he be in a calm judicial good-humor—whereas I *hate* travel, & I *hate* hotels, & I *hate* the opera, & I *hate* the Old Masters—in truth I don't ever seem to be in a good enough humor with ANY-thing to satirize it; no, I want to stand up before it & *curse* it, & foam at the mouth,—or take a club & pound it to rags and pulp" (*MTHL* 1:248–49). By the time the manuscript was at the printers, the *Tramp* had become for Mark Twain "that most infernally troublesome book" (*MTHL* 1:290). Its illustrations gave him trouble, he was fighting Canadian pirates, he had numerous other speaking, writing, and business obligations that kept him on edge, his family had been steadily on the move, Livy had been ill, and he himself had endured bouts of rheumatism and dysentery.

The result was a typically uneven performance, with some first-rate anecdotes, such as "Jim Baker's Bluejay Yarn," but also long mechanical stretches and a good deal of filler, especially in the latter reaches where others' accounts of Alpine climbing exploits and accidents were copied out verbatim. The tone is sometimes casual and

1. Their itinerary is detailed in *N&J2*, 46–49.

cheerfully irreverent, sometimes irritable and contemptuous. Overall, the composition is loose, as Mark Twain ac-
knowledged when after a digression of some fifteen pages
he began chapter nineteen: "However, I wander from the
raft" (171). Such casual devices opened the narrative to any
anarchistic invention, which liberated his imagination but
also permitted numerous pointless and mediocre pages. At
its best, the *Tramp* has such inspired stories as booking passage for Zermatt on a glacier, discovering after a night's
sleep that it has not moved, and deciding that it must have
run aground (454). But elsewhere, Twain was so distracted
or uninterested that he included the flattest of anecdotes.

Despite the maddening swamp of detail in which Mark
Twain found himself immersed, he responded enthusiastically to the order and efficiency of German life. Although he regarded Germans as warmhearted "children of
impulse," for him they were admirably well-behaved children (93). Despite the gory wounds they produced, their
dueling clubs mesmerized him. He admired the fortitude
of the young male participants, especially in comparison
with the French. Their artificial, histrionic dueling practices roused him to heights of savage comedy when he
described an imaginary duel between M. Gambetta and
M. Fourtou. (Leon Gambetta was the well-known contemporary French republican; "Fourtou" probably is a variant
on *foutu,* a vulgarism meaning, approximately, "done for"
or, more directly, "screwed.") The conclusion of that duel
was that Gambetta collapsed backward onto Twain, with
the result that Twain was "the only man who had been hurt
in a French duel in forty years" (80, 82). French civilization always seemed degradingly effeminate to Twain. He
thought Louis XVI "contemptible" as a king for having
been no better than a "female saint" in his conduct. As in
the *Innocents,* Twain preferred forceful masculine action.
Had Napoleon been in Louis's place, Twain remarks, the
Swiss guards would never have been massacred. And al-

though they would have no memorial today, still "there would be a well-stocked Communist graveyard in Paris which would answer just as well to remember the 10th of August by" (261).

Given such aggressive ferocity, one can see why Mark Twain turned by preference to German culture. Throughout the *Tramp,* he placed a series of German legends, some authentic, some invented. Almost all of them involve romantic or marital love in which the men are saved by, betrayed by, or do injury to women. The problems of the first, "The Knave of Bergen," are unusually interesting. The legend involves a knight encased in black armor who appears at a royal masked ball. His dancing and conversation please the queen, but when he is obliged to unmask, he turns out to be the executioner of Bergen. Enraged by his presumption, the king orders him to be executed, but the executioner argues (not very coherently or plausibly) that since the punishment will not expunge the ostensible disgrace, the king should knight him instead. The king does so, uttering a sentence of ineffable incoherence: "Well then, and gave him the knight-stroke, so I raise you to nobility, who begged for grace for your offense now kneels before me, rise as a knight" (21).

I can think of no justification for including a story so lamely concluded save that Mark Twain, the Westerner who had stormed the bastions of Eastern culture with his audacity, felt an affinity with the knave-executioner. A jester, who had married far above his station (Livy's father, a wealthy coal dealer, being the king, as it were, of Elmira, New York), he had become the part owner of a newspaper and had gained entrance to the central repository of culture, the *Atlantic Monthly.* In one undiplomatic speech, he had mocked the elders of the cultural pantheon, to the distress of Howells and even at times of himself. He was an untrustworthy barbarian, a knave, and in one sense of the

book's title, a "tramp"—a vagabond, a ne'er-do-well—
abroad. In an unused preface to the book, Twain confirmed
a modified version of this association. "I perceived that in
using the word Tramp I was unconsciously describing the
walker as well as the walk" (*MTLP,* 109–10).

If the presence of "The Knave of Bergen" is most easily
accounted for as a psychologically compelling analogue to
Twain, on other occasions Twain could fuse his own sense
of the world's constitution in objective and controlled art.
"Jim Baker's Bluejay Yarn" is as finely accomplished as any
tale Twain ever wrote. A blue jay, sprightly and intelligent,
discovers a hole in which he might store acorns. Unfortunately, the hole is in the roof of a cabin, so that hard as he
works to fill it up, he never succeeds. But as he has rea-
soned the project out for himself as plausible, he stub-
bornly keeps working at it. "Well, you're a long hole, and a
deep hole, and a mighty singular hole altogether—but I've
started in to fill you, and I'm d——d if I *don't* fill you, if it
takes a hundred years!" (39–40). Eventually, the reality is
discovered, whereupon all his fellow jays laugh wildly at
"the whole absurdity of the contract that that first jay had
tackled" (41).

This story also parallels Mark Twain's own activities and
temperament. He worked himself to distraction on projects
as ill conceived as the jay's. Estimating, for example, that *A
Tramp Abroad* required twenty-six hundred pages of manuscript, he wrote almost four thousand to achieve that length,
discarding many of them. (*MTB,* 663, 650). Such prodigious expenditures of energy were typical of his com-
positional habits. Of an uncompleted narrative, "Simon
Wheeler," Twain wrote Howells in 1898: "I didn't finish the
story, though I re-began it in several new ways, & spent altogether 70,000 words on it, then gave it up & threw it
aside" (*MTHL* 2:674–75). And throughout the eighties he
was investing in the prototype for the Paige typesetter,

sometimes throwing as much as two thousand dollars a month down that bottomless hole, until by 1894 he finally bankrupted himself.

The example of the ant suggested to Mark Twain another satire on enormous energy expended to no practical end. Observing an ant at work in the Black Forest, Twain discovered the absurdity of regarding it as a model of industry. The ant seemed to have neither a plan nor common sense. Its actions were aimless, awkward, and, when it encountered a fellow ant, quarrelsome. To Twain the ant seemed to have no legitimacy as a "moral agent," and although it did have strength, so did a toadstool. A toadstool could burst out of the ground, lifting "twice its own bulk into the air." In fact, Twain mused, "ten thousand toadstools, with the right purchase, could lift a man, I suppose." Then the devastating query: "But what good would it do?" (219).

Although Mark Twain admired German industry, he also understood its limitations. The Black Forest farmhouses established in his mind the conjunction of wealth and excrement. Rich farmers had huge piles of manure before their front doors. "When we saw a stately accumulation, we said, 'here is a banker'" (210). The prevalence of this stinking treasure inspired the plot of a "Black Forest Novel." In it a worthy but poor young man desperately digs for roots and by chance strikes a manure mine—"a limitless Bonanza, of solid manure!" (212).

Such comic avatars of vitality as the blue jay, the ant, the toadstool, and the poor young man capture Mark Twain's own sense of the self engaged in the world's business. One works industriously but hopelessly like the blue jay trying to fill a hole; one works furiously but without a plan like the ant; one works powerfully but to no significant end, like the toadstool; and one works diligently like the poor young German and is delighted to find—excrement.

Sometimes the seemingly inescapable presence of excrement overwhelmed Mark Twain. Of the Swiss canton of Valais, he said, "Its alleys run liquid dung—these villages are the shackliest & vilest we have seen anywhere. This canton may be called the fundament of Switzerland" (*N&J*2, 148–49; also 167). In the *Tramp,* this journal entry becomes wading "ankle deep through the fertilizer-juice" of the "reeking lanes" of the village of Saint Nicholas (398–99, 403). This revulsion is turned into denominational hostility that is vented in the comic rage of Twain's fictional companion, Harris, "a rabid Protestant." He begins by saying that "in the Protestant cantons you never see such poverty and dirt and squalor as you do in this Catholic one; you never see the lanes and alleys flowing with foulness" (403). This initial observation quickly rises to condemnatory extravagance: Protestant cantons don't have lop-eared dogs. They have road signs, flower boxes, "acres of cats," and "you never see a speck of dirt on a Protestant glacier" (404). The subject of filth was very much on Twain's mind, then, especially "during this walk from St. Nicholas," which was for him the most offensive of the Catholic villages (486). Saint Nicholas himself had earlier proved to be an imposter, for Twain scourged him as a man who, although lauded as "the peculiar friend of children," had in fact deserted his own ten children to become a hermit (325).

Such a world was seriously distorted, but unable to discover why, Mark Twain again elected to satirize Christianity. He spoke with irritable contempt of "the cracked-pot clangor of the cheap church bells" in America on Sundays (401). Or, taking note of a grave in Switzerland, he observed that it held a farmer who had lost his balance while plowing and fell fifteen hundred feet, to which he adds a footnote: "This was on Sunday. M.T." (485). Shortly, he was reminded of a preacher's son who was enjoined to play "only things that are suitable to the Sabbath day." The father later looks in to see his children playing the Expulsion from Eden, with the son "standing in an imposing attitude . . . with a dark and deadly frown on his face. What was meant was very plain—he was personating the Deity!" (489).

But attacking Christianity was wearing thin for Mark Twain. The source of disharmony lay far beneath people's mindless rituals and superstitions. Twain inhabited a secular world that made such terrible demands on his energy and so lacerated his sensibilities that at times he could only snort with indignant laughter. But this world also threatened genuine dangers. Sometimes Twain responded to the manifest perils of the mountains with a wild, surrealistic humor: riding a glacier like a train; taking an enormous roped party on what was in effect a simple mountain stroll; ascending Mont Blanc by telescope (419–50, 454–57, 515–19).

At other times, though, he conceded the authentic horror of falling from heights. The latter part of the *Tramp* is filled with precipices over which various persons plunge to their deaths. Twain dwelt on a scene of an old climber examining a sack containing the remains of friends who had dropped into and been absorbed by a glacier forty years earlier: " 'This is Balmat's hand, I remember it so well!' and the old man bent down and kissed it reverently, then closed his fingers upon it in an affectionate grasp." (469). The grisly lugubriousness of this scene, which is actually illustrated in the original edition, may seem exaggerated. Yet it renders some of the distress Twain felt in the presence of a remorseless reality. Shortly he would experience analogous feelings as he took the trip down the Mississippi in search of lost time and comrades. As we shall see, his morbidity persisted—expanded in fact.

Another of Mark Twain's responses to nature's hostility to man was to create a sentimentally defiant image. The higher reaches of the Alps, with their lack of vegetation, struck him as a "grisly desert," a "smileless desolation" (371, 370). There was nothing, he said, "but death and desolation in these hideous places." Yet in the midst of "the most forlorn and arid and dismal" place of them all, he found a blue forget-me-not that impressed him as trying "to make a whole vast despondent Alpine desolation stop breaking its heart over the unalterable" (371). So he plucked it and sent it to a friend.[2]

Analogous images appear regularly in Mark Twain's writing. The party of miners lost in the Nevada snowstorm is almost next to a stage station (*RI,* chap. 33). In the *Tramp,* Twain places another party on the Rigi-Kulm mountainside, lost on a foggy night, seated miserably in a chill, muddy darkness, and terrified by a "vast body" that showed itself for an instant, like "the face of a precipice" (293–94). Ultimately, this fearful looming turned out to be the summit hotel. Twain was constantly trying to conjure away the terror of the void by laughing at it or by showing that the gallant little flower can outshine the dreariest landscape or that help is nearby, would we only look. But he could never permanently dispel the apprehension that all these versions of relief were nonsense.

The Rigi-Kulm presented a series of related experiences of comic frustration. Here Mark Twain once again set a goal—to enjoy "that wonderful spectacle, an Alpine sunrise"—that he then failed to achieve. On the first attempt, "fagged out" by the arduous climb, he and his companion sleep in a halfway station until "half past three in the afternoon," thereby missing the sunrise and suffering "a bit-

2. Cf. Walter Blair's remark: "Although the passage is marred when Twain has the flower chirrup inane advice about cheering up, by then it has embodied his dilemma pictorially. Otherwise its emotional freighting is a puzzle" (*Mark Twain and Huck Finn* [Berkeley, 1962], 344).

ter disappointment" (290–91). They continue to climb, though, until they reach the summit hotel, where again they fall exhausted into bed. Awakened the next morning by an Alpine horn, they rush out to a viewing platform and ecstatically contemplate the sun just above the mountain-tops, until they suddenly realize that it is going down instead of coming up. They had again slept through the day and were now watching a sunset (299). On their third try to see a sunrise, they notice only a delicate lightening of the atmosphere. After puzzling over this phenomenon, they realize that they have been looking at the western, rather than the eastern, horizon (302).

This series of misadventures is offered as spirited farce, but one can discern an underlying significance: dawn, rising expectations, hope, a fresh beginning—all these promises of America were denied Mark Twain because he had arrived too late, because he had mistaken one phenomenon for another, because he had looked in the wrong direction. For a man as intent on establishing and advancing himself as Twain, this particular frustration had a special poignancy because, although others might judge him to have achieved a spectacular success, in his own mind he remained uneasy and insecure. He seemed doomed to misunderstand the rules of the game, supposing there were any. As he observed in his notebook in May 1879: "When I get beyond 6 times 7 is 35 I'm done" (*N&J*2, 310). Later that rueful note would be attributed to his shrewd but equally beleaguered and largely helpless young hero Huck Finn.

Lacking a philosophy, a system, or even a set of conventions that he could both respect and effectively use in the conduct of life, Mark Twain mocked a number of conventional practices available to him in his more narrow role as a writer, for to his mind they represented illusory ways of organizing and controlling the mercurial world. Various literary subgenres are parodied through the *Tramp*. An "Official Report of a Visit to the Furka Region," for example, is punctuated throughout with foreign terms: "The *wlgw* was very severe; our sleeping place could hardly be *distingueè* from the snow around it, which had fallen to the depth of a *flirk* during the past evening, and we heartily enjoyed a rough scramble *en bas* to the Giesbach Falls" (319). Why employ such verbal rubbish? "To adorn my page," Twain replies. "They all do it." Who is "all"? "Everybody. Everybody that writes elegantly" (321).

Although Mark Twain scorches such pretentiousness, he is capable of satirizing its polar opposite, the writer who lacks a specific vocabulary and so substitutes an all-purpose term when needed—in this instance, *thing*. The subject is the European manner of harnessing a horse: "The man stands up the horses on each side of the thing that projects from the front end of the wagon, and then throws the tangled mess of gear on top of the horses, and passes the thing that goes forward through a ring, and hauls it aft, and passes the other thing through the other thing" (329).

Mark Twain also mocks the jargon of the fashion world, describing the costume of a Swiss waitress that "consists of a single gros de laine, trimmed with ashes of roses, with overskirt of sacre bleu ventre saint gris, cut bias on the off side" (340). Similarly, Twain reflected irreverently, in scientific language, on the clear mountain air: "I had a theory that the gravitation of refraction, being subsidiary to atmospheric compensation, the refrangibility of the earth's surface would emphasize this effect in regions where great mountain ranges occur, and possibly so even-handedly impact the odic and idyllic forces together, the one upon the other, as to prevent the moon rising higher than 12,200 feet above sea level" (507).

These parodies all concern systems of language and attitude that have become sufficiently mechanical and materialistic to merit satirical dismissal. The ease with which they pretended to convey truth in fact concealed reality. Given Mark Twain's persistent probing after final truths, his parodies are ultimately serious critiques. An accurate match of language and experience, Twain believed, would provide him access to reality, and for the main part of his career he dedicated himself to trying to find the right voice to convey his perceptions.

That search for accuracy often turned to associations. Following them involved exploratory travel through the mind's landscape, well off the standard tourist itineraries. Rhetorical form distorted reality. The mind could be taught to follow accepted verbal patterns so that language could be used as a pragmatic instrument. Most people, for economic as well as psychological reasons, had therefore to adapt their verbalizing to a narrow range of expression. They neither had the time to reconcile in words any apparently eccentric reactions they had, nor were they in a position to display the peculiar disorderliness of their thinking processes, even though in times of passion or intoxication or weariness, when the inner monitors had temporarily relaxed their vigilance, evidence of such mental unruliness might reveal itself. Otherwise, only such persons as the child, the self-sufficient rural figure, the worker without hope of advancement, the outlaw who had already consciously repudiated social conventions, the rich who had inherited or gained immunity, and the cantankerous old— only those felt free enough "to speak their minds."

Still, full relaxation of the filtering and channeling mechanisms in the mind that selected appropriate verbal responses and arranged them in communicable order was likely to constitute a symptom of madness. The "word-salads" of certain forms of schizophrenia illustrate arbitrary verbal associations powerful and persistent enough for society to judge the speaker mentally incapacitated. Nonetheless, in this century radical versions of the mind verbalizing have been explored in conspicuously central works. James Joyce represented some thought processes in colloquial clusters of truncated associations, whereas Gertrude Stein produced austerely subjective records of her verbal reactions to the objects in her immediate world. Further, much work on the possibilities of language has been carried on by poets, philosophers, linguists, and literary critics in this century, leading to a general awareness that verbalization is a symbolic, not a mimetic, activity. The human agent wishes to give apprehensible form to certain inchoate feelings and images, but the medium of the language necessarily adapts these mental materials to its own special structures. Such adaptations involve selection rather than detailed imitations, for nothing verbal could provide an accurate model of anything mental. The verbal rendition becomes something symbolic standing for something else in the consciousness. In short, portions of the subject are selected and inevitably distorted in order to represent the whole.

Associations serve as bridges from one part of reality to another. In the metaphoric act, the aggressive, powerful behavior of a warrior has long been compared to that of a lion. Even in its usually abbreviated expression ("He is a lion") the comparison, although trite by now, is susceptible to analysis and extension. Reflecting on the attributes of a lion, one might develop further associations: he is handsome; he is proud; he is protective. Such associations are confined in a fixed channel, though, one meant to convey the strength and nobility of the warrior.

Other associations are available as well, but because they threaten to destroy the carefully guarded image, they are normally suppressed. On the other hand, for the humorist they are gifts. In drawing out the suppressed parts of a metaphor, Mark Twain discovered both humor and a source of fresh perspectives. Suppose the metaphoric comparison of warrior to lion were elaborated: "He copulates twenty times a day," or "He lets the female do the work," or "He roars a lot, then goes to sleep." Any of these comparisons does accurately describe the behavior of the male lion, but because they all furnish unexpected and irreverent perspectives on the subject, they are liable to strike us as funny. Equally important, though, such unconventional associations may also afford another way of understanding some part of the world. Like lions, men of power often do gather a harem about them and let underlings do most of their work. Toward the end of Twain's life, men like Zola, Frank Norris, and Dreiser were actually presenting versions of that reality, although not as humor.

The unexpected images of humor often implicitly criticize not only the person being treated irreverently but also overused images and language. Mark Twain habitually selected "inappropriate" associations to set off explosions of humor. When he was on the lecture platform, his employment of the theatrical pause enhanced the effect. As he stood there, silently ruminating, the audience could feel him sorting through various possible phrasings until at last, in mischievous triumph, he selected the observation that was unexpected but revealingly right. For example, at his seventieth birthday dinner, observed that he had "always bought cheap cigars—reasonably cheap, at any rate. Sixty years ago they cost me four dollars a barrel, but my taste has improved, latterly, and I pay seven now. Six or seven. Seven, I think. Yes, it's seven. But that includes the barrel" (*MTSp,* 258–59).

At times the unconventional association could misfire. After having described imposters who had identified themselves as Longfellow, Emerson, and Holmes at the Whittier birthday dinner, Twain recalled that "now, then, the house's *attention* continued, but the expression of interest in the

faces turned to a sort of black frost. I wondered what the
trouble was. I didn't know" (*MTSp*, 71). That was the rare
occasion when he had misjudged his audience, but in entering unfamiliar areas Twain risked such misjudgments. In
"How To Tell a Story," he argued that "to string incongruities and absurdities together in a wandering and sometimes purposeless way, and seem innocently unaware that
they are absurdities, is the basis of the American art, if my
position is correct."[3] This activity he sometimes attributed
to a simple, guileless narrator, whose wandering consciousness was easily diverted into new subjects far from
the narrative's main road. But he himself also played a version of that role in his public persona. On the lecture platform his delivery was "peculiarly slow." Paul Fatout has
characterized Twain's casual manner as differing from the
vigorous norm of speakers of his day. "Chatting conversa-
tionally, wrinkling up his nose and half closing his eyes, he
lounged loosely upon and around the desk, occasionally
marching and counter-marching for a short space, once in
awhile vaguely gesturing with one hand, or quizzically
pulling his mustache. In these ways he varied so much from
the conventional that critics called him eccentric."[4] One
can see how this casual strolling through the associative by-
ways of the mind became analogous to traveling. One may
have an itinerary but is nonetheless always ready for side
adventures, even though they turn out to be dead ends, or
dangerous. More often than not, though, the result is en-
tertainingly revealing, as when Twain refuses to fall into
raptures before Leonardo's *Last Supper* because he sees the
grotesque abuse and deterioration of the painting.

Occasionally he pushed further, trying out other possi-

3. In *How to Tell a Story and Other Essays* (New York, 1900), 11.
4. Paul Fatout, *Mark Twain on the Lecture Circuit* (Bloomington, Ind., 1960), 86, 76.

bilities, quite unsystematically and without coming to any
logical closure, for this was where the associative path led
him. However bizarre and disconcerting such moments
might be, he allowed them entrance to his page, for they
represented a faithful record of the movement of his mind
through its unregulated complexities. Sometimes these associations established authentic relations among otherwise
disparate subjects. When he encountered children playing
at mountain climbing on a manure pile (improbably "roped
together with a string" and carrying "mimic alpenstocks
and ice-axes"), they reminded him of children in Nevada
playing at silver mining. In these games, he recalled, there
were always two "star roles, the one who fell down the
shaft, and the one who rescued him" (487). This memory
of role playing generated by the sight of the Swiss children
on a manure pile in turn reminded Twain of the preacher's
son who played the part of a disapproving God, scowling
at his younger sisters, enacting the expulsion from Eden
(488–89).

By describing these scenes that were related in his mind,
Mark Twain managed to produce two more printed pages
as he drove himself irritably to complete what had begun to
seem an interminable book. The three topics are not particularly funny or original, but for our purposes they accurately display associative connections as well as underlying
concerns in Twain's mind. In the past four years he had published *Tom Sawyer* and had worked on both *Huckleberry
Finn* and *The Prince and the Pauper,* which is to say that
Twain's imagination was already inhabiting the realm of
childhood and its fantasies. We also know that the op-
pressiveness of American Christianity was a persistent obsession for him. Sunday in America meant to him "stay in
the house and keep still." By contrast, "Sunday is the great
day on the continent,—the free day, the happy day" (231).
The little boy who assumed the role of God had first pre-

tended he was driving horsecars; then he played at being a steamboat captain, then at leading an army. But each time, his father stopped him, insisting that the boy should only do what was suitable for Sunday, which, as it turned out, was to play God with that "dark and deadly frown on his face." Twain's comment: "Think of the guileless sublimity of that idea." Then, absolved from further comment by the looseness of the travel book's format, he abruptly starts a new paragraph: "We reached Vispach at 8 p.m., only about seven hours out from St. Nicholas" (489).

Once the *Tramp* was under way, Mark Twain made an overt point of acknowledging the casualness of his narrative by remarking after telling an anecdote, "But I digress" (345). In fact, though, even at their most abrupt moments his associative sequences still exhibit a degree of mechanical coherence. Having, for example, recounted the legend of a crusader who mistakenly killed his beloved while she was singing, Twain begins the next chapter: "The last legend reminds one of the 'Lorelei.'" This rudimentary signal of a mental relation permits him then to tell the story of the Lorelei; to provide Heine's lyric in German, plus the music for it; to offer his own translation of Heine's poem, which he then compares with an atrocious rendering by another; to provide a series of bizarre sentences drawn from a picture catalogue that was "written in a peculiar kind of English" (like the translation); and finally to bring the chapter to a serenely arbitrary conclusion: "But meantime the raft is moving on" (140–49).

"The last legend reminds one of the 'Lorelei.'" To be *re*-minded is literally to be drawn back into the mind, there to follow other branching attachments. If the relations are subjective, like Proust's madeleine generating images out of the involuntary memory, for the perceiver they are no less authentic. The compelling seductiveness of such relations for Twain was that· they often involved subjects of the greatest power for him, namely sex, suffering, and death. He addressed them regularly in his work, but never, for him, satisfactorily. Following associative logic, though, gave him entrance to the underworld of his mind. At the same time, yielding to the stimulus of the Lorelei of association involved dangers for a writer comparable to those run by any seaman hypnotized by her song. In Twain's translation: "He sees not the yawning breakers, / He sees but the maid alone: / The pitiless billows engulf him!— / So perish the sailor and the bark" (146). The associative Lorelei threatened to engulf him in the tumultuous ocean of the mind. But the seduction of her voice was strong.

As the years passed, Mark Twain struggled intellectually with his dissatisfactions in what he called his "Gospel," *What Is Man?* Concerned lest its unorthodox ideas injure his public reputation, he finally published it anonymously, not even allowing it "to be copyrighted in his name."[5] In this book, he tried to convince himself that man was not responsible for the contents of his mind, or for his behavior. As the wisdom figure, the Old Man, says: "No man ever originates anything. All his thoughts, all his impulses come from the *outside*" (*WIM,* 129). The Old Man's pupil, a Young Man, is set an exercise to demonstrate that if he were to leave his mind "to its own devices it would find things to think about without any of my help, and thus convince me that it was a machine" (181). The Young Man then describes a classic associative sequence that occurred while he was shaving: an image of a yellow cat comes spontaneously to his mind; it reminds him of a cat he once saw in boyhood in a church, which had become tangled in flypaper to the amusement of the congregation; the spectators, suppressing their laughter, produced tears; those tears reminded the Young Man of a Darwinian story in which a father in Tierra

5. Hamlin Hill, *Mark Twain: God's Fool* (New York, 1975), 131.

del Fuego hurled his child against some rocks, whereupon the weeping mother took the dying child to her breast. Finally, the most personal association for Twain and at the same time the least explicable, for it has no link, comes when the Young Man recalls "an ever-recurring and disagreeable dream of mine. In this dream I always find myself, stripped to my shirt, cringing and dodging about in the midst of a great drawingroom throng of finely dressed ladies and gentlemen, and wondering how I got there." With that, the Young Man summarizes the phenomenon: "And so on and so on, picture after picture, incident after incident, a drifting panorama of ever-changing, ever-dissolving views manufactured by my mind without any help from me" (181–82).

The uncontrolled action of the mind is accurately rendered here, even though with "and so on and so on" the rendition stops just at the edge of the most problematic situation. Twain famously broke through the barrier to forbidden material once in the winter of 1896–1897, when in his notebook he recorded a dream he had had of "a negro wench," eating "a mushy apple pie—hot." He purchased a pie for himself. She then made him "a disgusting proposition," and when he first countered sarcastically, then asked for a spoon, she took hers from her mouth and offered it to him, whereupon he awoke (*MTN,* 351–52).

If he could demonstrate that the mind operated mechanically, Mark Twain would be freed from any responsibility for its functioning. But the insufficiency of the solution he laboriously worked out in *What Is Man?* forced him to keep addressing the problem. This led him to dreams again, like those recorded in that series of fantasies printed posthumously in *Which Was the Dream?* Ultimately, though, the conclusion to "No. 44, The Mysterious Stranger" conceded his inability to comprehend the workings of his mind. All he could do was deny its reality. "*Nothing* exists," says the Satan figure; "all is a dream." Worse, that dream was "frankly and hysterically insane—like all dreams." The narrator is brought to perceive that "there is no God, no universe, no human race, no earthly life, no heaven, no hell. It is all a Dream, a grotesque and foolish dream" (*MSM*, 404–5). That was the desperate, nihilistic conclusion to which Twain was driven by his inability to fathom the governance of the mind.

Before he reached this end, though, he tried bravely, if sporadically, to find a way through the passages of his mental caverns without becoming irredeemably lost. His memory of the caves of his boyhood Hannibal reflects his image of the mind. From *Tom Sawyer* comes this description: McDougal's cave was "but a vast labyrinth of crooked aisles that ran into each other and out again and led nowhere. It was said that one might wander days and nights together through its intricate tangle of rifts and chasms, and never find the end of the cave; and that he might go down, and down, and still down, into the earth, and it was just the same—labyrinth underneath labyrinth, and no end to any of them. No man 'knew' the cave. That was an impossible thing" (204).

Even when he was not attempting to map the subterranean depths of his mind but was only ambling along in a casual way over its surface, Mark Twain enjoyed illustrating its quicksilver shifts. One chapter in the *Tramp* is explicitly dedicated to the pleasures of free-flowing conversation. The advantage of a pedestrian tour, Twain says, is that "there being no constraint, a change of subject is always in order" (221). In this instance, "constraint" represents social expectations and the requirements of business. Under relaxed circumstances, one more nearly approaches "naturalness," while at the same time there is an exploratory aspect to entering "the glad, free, boundless realm of things we were not certain about" (222).

Twain then illustrates the fertile proliferation of a day's

conversation. It begins with a discussion of awkward grammatical constructions that are compared in number to the milk teeth. This provides a transition to the subject of dentistry. Both subjects had been presaged in the prologue to this episode by Twain's progression from "talking" to "the movement of the tongue" to "the wagging of the gladsome jaw," although he does not seem aware of this developing imagery of the mouth (221). In any case, the talk then passes successively through various topics until it reaches a long anecdote concerning a skeleton placed by pranksters in a bed to frighten a young bumpkin, Nicodemus Dodge. Although the distance is considerable between the onset of the conversation and this point, Twain insists on the underlying coherence of the sequence: "By a logical process the conversation melted out of one of these subjects and into the next" (223).

We possess the notebook entries in which this chapter began. First came a long entry concerning Mark Twain's pain from having bitten down too hard on a grape seed. This may eventually have suggested the whole complex of imagery involving the mouth. Then comes a line on Nicodemus Dodge. Finally, he puts down an example of the grammatically impacted sentence with which this sequence in the *Tramp* begins (*N&J*2, 137–38).

We can see two kinds of associative writing operating in this chapter. The first is overtly mechanical: "Dental surgeons suggested doctors, doctors suggested death, death suggested skeletons" (223). The second is deeper, more personal, and unconnected with this particular conversation in any obvious way. During this period Mark Twain was regularly immersing himself in what Henry Nash Smith has called "the matter of Hannibal." [6] So it is not by chance that the skeleton referred to in the associative se-

---

6. Henry Nash Smith, *Mark Twain: Development of a Writer* (Cambridge, Mass., 1962), 74.

quence is said to be that of "Jimmy Finn, the village drunk-
ard" who had sold his own bones when he "lay very sick in
the tanyard a fortnight before his death" (228). That image
had long been in Twain's memory, for he had written about
Jimmy Finn as early as 1867 in a dispatch to the *Alta California*. There, Finn "sold his body to a doctor for a quart of
whiskey."[7] This strong personal linkage in Twain's mind
between the specific person Jimmy Finn and the image of a
skeleton explains how Jimmy Finn entered the anecdote of
Nicodemus Dodge, even though the associative connection is not available in the *Tramp* itself.

The mind's vagaries were always a compelling subject
for Mark Twain. If they were an important source of his
humor, they also hinted at epistemological revelations. In
"Old Times on the Mississippi," for example, he described
at length a pilot named Brown who could forget nothing.
He remembered not only the contours of the river that es-
caped the young Twain but everything else as well. This
made him tedium exemplified, for his narratives were
clogged with detail. He could not tell a straight story.
Twain outlines the unraveling of a typical Brown account
where the narrative "drifts," where one detail calls up another, where "pork and hay would suggest corn and fodder; corn and fodder would suggest cows and horses; cows
and horses would suggest the circus and certain celebrated
bare-back riders; the transition from the circus to the me-
nagerie was easy and natural; from the elephant to equa-
torial Africa was but a step; then of course the heathen sav-
ages would suggest religion" (*LOM,* 86).[8]

7. Walter Blair, *Mark Twain and Huck Finn,* 11.

8. In "Mark Twain: The Writer as Pilot," Edgar J. Burde argues that whereas "Old Times on the Mississippi" represents the
intuitive authority of Bixby's memory, the *lack* of control in the
later part of *Life on the Mississippi* is reflected in the indiscrimi-

Now manifestly Mark Twain was here describing his own sense of the mind's wayward functioning, except that by unrelenting development he had elevated the pilot's infirmity to a caricature of actual experience. As Brown tediously and mechanically recapitulates the past, he becomes the target of the humor. Yet the very looseness of an associative narrative constitutes one of Mark Twain's creative triumphs—the story of grandfather's old ram (*RI*, chap. 53). In "Old Times," Brown superficially sounds like Jim Blaine. "And the said Captain Hardy wore yarn socks winter and summer just the same, and his first wife's name was Jane Shook—she was from New England—and his second one died in a lunatic asylum" (74). But even though the associative method is similar, the richness of Blaine's imagination as well as the color of his dialect is missing from the pilot's speech. Mark Twain never soared higher than in his creation of Blaine's warm, interested, kindly mind. "Old Squire Hogadorn could carry around more mixed licker, and cuss better than most any man I ever see. His second wife was the widder Billings—she that was Becky Martin—her dam was Deacon Dunlap's first wife. Her oldest child, Maria, married a missionary and died in grace—et up by the savages. They et *him,* too, poor fellow—biled him" (*RI,* 347).

The intentions of the pilot Brown and of Jim Blaine are identical. Each undertakes to discuss a subject—a dog, a ram—yet never reaches it. But Brown constructs his narrative by mechanical addition, whereas Blaine practices a fertile multiplication. Twain had difficulty, though, in gaining any sustained access to this method, for what could jus-

---

nately littered mind of the pilot, Brown (*PMLA* 93, no. 5 [October, 1978]: 887). In "Mark Twain: The Pilot and the Writer," Edgar M. Branch vigorously contests this argument (*Mark Twain Journal* 23, no. 2 [Fall 1985]: 28–43).

tify it? In the case of Brown, the justification was his character as an unimaginative bore, possessed with total recall.
Blaine's wandering memory was unleashed by alcohol.
And in the *Tramp,* the casual circumstance of a forest stroll
with a friend encouraged the free flow of associations. But
the motivation for each of these associative flows was particular, unique. The associative technique remained largely
unavailable to Mark Twain.

Associations can also be present but unacknowledged or
even unrealized by the author. These last constitute a more
complicated area for interpretation. Although some of
Mark Twain's references and images are reasonably comprehensible, others are at best obscurely provocative. As an
example involving literal images, Mark Twain elected to
make half a dozen or so drawings for the *Tramp,* initially
intending them as one of the book's running jokes. As he
wrote Twichell: "I shall make from 10 to 20 illustrations for
my book with my own (almighty rude and crude) pencil,
and shall say in the title page that some of the pictures in the
book are from original drawings by the author. I have already made two or three which suit me. It gives me a belly-
ache to look at them" (*MTLP,* 111). After enumerating the
illustrators who contributed to the *Tramp,* its title page
does add "with also three or four pictures made by the author of this book, without outside help." But it must be
said that none of them seems particularly amusing, and
most are not only technically crude but also virtually meaningless. I cannot pretend, then, to offer much interpretative
help with them. Nonetheless, their enigmatic presences
should be mentioned, for although Mark Twain mocked
his lack of artistic skill throughout his career, he persisted
in printing his atrocious sketches.

Here, he offers a drawing of a man on a tower, where the
sizes are disproportionate, and a lively one of a horse drawing a wagon full of passengers, in which "several blem-

ishes" still remain (104–5, 125). He is confident, however, about having solved the problems of his first subject: "The man on top, looking at the view, is apparently too large, but I found he could not be made smaller, conveniently. I wanted him there, and I wanted him visible, so I thought out a way to manage it; I composed the picture from two points of view; the spectator is to observe the man from about where the flag is, and he must observe the tower itself from the ground. This harmonizes the seeming discrepancy" (104–5). In the book, he makes an ironic point of his artistic gifts. "My study of Art in Heidelberg has been a noble education to me. All that I am to-day in Art, I owe to that" (563; see also 100).

Several of the drawings in the *Tramp* represent something broken. For example, the first is entitled "piece of sword." It is supposedly a line drawing of a portion of a sword fractured in a duel, made by "tracing a line around it with my pen" (68). That being approximately what it appears to be, and no more, the source of humor remains obscure. Equally banal are his drawings of an Etruscan tear-jug with a hole in it and a cracked Henry II plate.

These are followed by a full page printed in facsimile of the manuscript, discussing a small drawing of a cat and a mouse in the upper left-hand corner of the page (185–86). These figures supposedly represent a valuable ceramic piece, but why Twain reproduced his handwriting, let alone the drawing itself, is lost somewhere in his psyche. He did like cats. And the concluding reference to "the Chung-a-Lung-Fung dynasty" does offer faint echoes of male drinking (Chug-a-lug) and of sexual engagement ("Fung"), but these are thin and dubious responses. What, then, was Twain's intention? His presentation is so loose that one is not even sure whether the cat and unmentioned mouse are intended as ceramic objects or as designs on a ceramic piece.

Two other inexplicable drawings appear on a single page. Purporting to show rafts on the Neckar River from above, they invite the imagination to interpret them, especially the lower, but without assistance, so that one must conclude that these drawings either verge on the forbidden or are exceedingly insignificant.

Mark Twain's notebooks offer no clue to the meaning of these drawings, except in one case. In his notebook he drew a sketch of the Jungfrau, where the peak appears between two other, rounded, peaks (not unlike elevated knees) with a decided nipple on its tip (*N&J*2, 141). When he rendered the drawing for the book, he altered it slightly: the side peaks were crosshatched, trees were added to the top of the one on the left, and the prominence of the nipple was reduced (346). One can never be altogether sure whether private or inadvertently created associations have led one to attribute meaning where it does not exist. Here, however, the name Jungfrau encourages anatomical interpretation. Further, we know that such associations were in Twain's mind on this trip. A pair of towers on a Munich cathedral stirred the following response in his notebook: "Frauenkirche— cow-teats" (*N&J*2, 318).

Old Blue China.

I also set apart my exquisite specimen of Old Blue China. This is considered to be the finest example of Chinese art now in existence; I do not refer to the bastard Chinese art of modern times but that noble & pure & genuine art which flourished under the fostering & appreciative care of the Emperors of the Chung-a Lung-Fung dynasty. —

Bird waiting for a Fish, a
Common Spectacle.
(Perspective of Bird not Correct.)

Raft coming down between Stone Dikes.

Raft curving itself through
crooked piece of River. (Merely
a Study, not a finished
picture)

In general, despite the breadth of his experience, Mark Twain accepted the prohibitions of his adopted society against sexual references in literature, yet he chafed against them. In the *Tramp,* he complained vociferously about the differing moral standards that society demanded of literature as opposed to painting and sculpture. "Art is allowed as much indecent license to-day as in earlier times—but the privileges of literature in this respect have been sharply curtailed within the past eighty or ninety years" (577). This accords with his observation in his notebook: "By far the *very* funniest things that ever happened or were ever said are unprintable (in our day). A great pity. It was no so [*sic*] in the freer day of Boccacio [*sic*] & Rabelais" (*N&J*2, 87). A few moments later, having remembered an anecdote that amuses him, he counseled himself: "Try the whole story, with dashes to represent swearing & obscenity" (*N&J*2, 87). In the *Tramp* passage, he went on to say that "Fielding and Smollett could portray the beastliness of their day in the beastliest language," whereas contemporary writers might not, not even when they used "nice and guarded forms of speech" (577). Although Twain appears to be speaking on behalf of freedom of expression, to do so in terms of "indecent license" and "beastliness" signals his own reservations about unmonitored expression.

Such ideas lead Mark Twain to a specific diatribe of considerable and surprising violence concerning Titian's painting, the *Venus of Urbino*. The first draft in his notebook had called her "purely the Goddess of the Beastly (Bestial)" (*N&J*2, 319). But because the fingers of her left hand quite explicitly rested between her legs on her mons, Twain indignantly expanded this reaction for the book to say that Titian had painted "the foulest, the vilest, the obscenest picture the world possesses" (578). There's no humor here, no distance to his outrage. Nor, although couched in this

form, is this essentially a plea for greater liberty of expression in literature. Twain thought he disapproved of censorship, but in most matters he willingly tolerated it.

These issues were too powerful and complicated for Twain to have thought through. In her diary in 1906, his secretary, Isabel Lyon, recorded that Twain had told her, concerning his autobiography, that "there were the Rousseau confessions, but I am going to leave that kind alone, for Rousseau had looked after that end."[9] In his later private life and writing he tended to be silent about or to disapprove of license in sexual matters. It's worth noting that whatever its public reputation, *1601* is much more scatological than pornographic. Twain preferred to leave sexual irregularity to the French. They, he told his notebook, were "the nation of the filthy-minded." They have, he thought, "bestialities which are unknown in civilized lands" (*N&J*2, 323).

Whipsawed by such contradictory impulses as this desire to have the artistic freedom of a painter yet also feeling that a public representation of sexual behavior was corrupt, Mark Twain turned with relief in the *Tramp* to an account of a raft trip on the Neckar. The account was long, extending some sixty pages (123–83). Yet the trip never took place. Twain did make a voyage by boat on the Neckar from Heilbronn to Hirschhorn on August 9, 1878 (the itinerary is in *N&J*2, 47), but the only related entry reads: "At this castle passed a raft" (*N&J*2, 134). However, the *idea* of a raft on a river remained profoundly important to Twain. Not the piloting of a steamboat, though. The world of the raft for Huck and Jim was first evoked in Twain's writing in the summer of 1876 in the early chapters of *Huckleberry*

9. Hamlin Hill, *Mark Twain: God's Fool,* 136.

Finn. He permitted reality to intrude violently in chapter 16, however, by having a steamboat smash through the raft. When he took up the manuscript again sometime between the spring of 1880 and the summer of 1883, he produced the familiar idyllic description of raft life: "We said there ain't no home like a raft, after all. Other places do seem so cramped up and smothery, but a raft don't. You feel mighty free and easy and comfortable on a raft" (chap. 18).

In the *Tramp* the raft is similarly extolled. Its gentle, gliding, noiseless motion makes existence "a dream, a charm, a deep and tranquil ecstasy" (126). But the destructive impulse was in him too, for just before he decides to take a raft trip, he says that he had been sitting "for hours," watching rafts on the river below, "hoping to see one of them hit the bridge-pier and wreck itself sometime or other, but was always disappointed" (124). And the imaginary trip finally concludes in a glorious, destructive collision, engineered by Mark Twain himself. The calamity he had so fervently hoped to observe, he created by stepping ashore just as the raft headed straight for a bridge. "The next moment I had my long coveted desire: I saw a raft wrecked. It hit the pier in the center and went all to smash and scatteration like a box of matches struck by lightning" (182–83). One will not often see quite so baldly dramatized the opposing needs for placidity and action, for passive drift and aggressive destruction, but both were central to Mark Twain's personality, and the travel book afforded him the imaginative space in which to gratify these psychological needs.

As Mark Twain pulled the *Tramp* together, he was in a typical frenzy of activity, trying to master his professional life. April 15, 1879: "Perkins says your father didn't promise to get my stock out of the Pub. Co. free of loss. I ain't prepared to say he did—and I wouldn't want him to do a thing he couldn't do, anyway. But I want him to get rid of all of my stock but about 5 or 10 shares at the best figure he can before he leaves the concern. What is that stock worth, now?" (*MTLP*, 112). May 10, 1879: "Our government will charge 25 per cent duty on the cost of the *plates,* nothing on the artist's work. (I have been consulting the law, at the consulate.) This will add $125 or $150 to the total cost (I don't know what the freight will be on a box of plates,)—and the total cost of the 210 pictures will then be, say, $1325 or $1350, *artist's work included*" (*MTLP*, 114). June 10, 1879: "All right—have just written Perkins that Tom Sawyer fills the Riley contract, and instructed him to have the Co endorse all my contracts as completed and deduct $2000 from copyrights now due, in satisfaction of the Riley debt" (*MTLP*, 116).

In the *Tramp,* the anecdote "The Man Who Put Up at Gadsby's" offers a counter to all such frantic efforts at controlling events in one's life. Gadsby's was a Washington hotel, and "to put up there" meant to "take it easy" rather than try to rush things through the processes of government. The story came to Mark Twain as he was exercising his own patience while waiting to see a fisherman actually catch a fish from the lake at Lucerne. He then remembered a friend suggesting comparable patience once to a young man who had come to Washington to obtain a postmastership. The friend tells the story of a man who cheerfully accepted endless delays in getting action from the federal government. The young man listens to the story of the protracted stay at Gadsby's, then asks: "But what's it all *for?*" The answer is a fundamental one for Twain: "O, nothing in particular." The young man presses for the relevance of accepting delay: "Well, where's the point of it?" The answer comes blandly: "O, there isn't any particular point to it" (270). Therefore it is generally best to meet the frustrations of life by putting up at Gadsby's—that is, by being patient and not pushing for immediate results or looking for any meaning to one's frustration.

Comparable patience is called for by parts of Mark Twain's travel writing. They don't yield meaning instantly, for there is no immediate point to them. Upon reflection, though, they sometimes do make sense if understood as expressions of his harried, pessimistic, highly articulate sensibility. For example, near the end of the book Twain contemplates the cathedral of Venice and praises it because he finds it out-and-out ugly, unlike most famous buildings, which are a "mixture of the ugly and the beautiful. . . . No misplaced and impertinent beauties are intruded anywhere; and the consequent result is a grand harmonious whole, of soothing, entrancing, tranquilizing, soul-satisfying ugliness." His conclusion is simply stated: "St Mark is perfect" (567). Is it mere happenstance that there is no possessive, that it doesn't read: "St Mark's [cathedral] is perfect"? I'm not inclined to think so.[10] The ironic self-sanctification and perfection (of consummate ugliness) is very much in Twain's sly style.

Such self-deprecation also appears in two jokes that Mark Twain reprints from the German humorous papers. They conclude the final appendix, and so the book as a whole. In the first, a "most dilapidated tramp" is seen contemplating some coins and concluding that the begging business is near its end. "Only about five marks ($1.25) for the whole day; many an official makes more!" (631). Here both the "tramp" and the "mark" are presented as of little moment.

The last anecdote concerns a "commercial traveler" (one definition of Mark Twain in his present role). He wishes to

10. In his notebook, it is "Saint Peter's," but usually "St. Mark," although on one occasion he does write "St. Mark's" (*N&J*2, 196, 197, 222).

show his samples to a merchant, but the merchant emphatically turns him away, upon which the salesman pleads, "But do you mind letting *me* look at them! I haven't seen them for three weeks!" (631). Which is to say that an exhausted and irritable Mark Twain elected to end his book with two weakly humorous anecdotes, both involving pathetically unsuccessful figures, a beggar and a salesman. Like himself, tramps abroad.

6

In the spring of 1882, Mark Twain made a trip down the Mississippi River to gather materials to complete the book begun as "Old Times on the Mississippi." He was unclear about the shape the book would take but did not follow through on a query in his notebook: "Begin with a chapter of my experiences as a *pilot?*" (*N&J2*, 457). Some trauma was still connected with the subject, for he also noted: "My nightmares, to this day, take the form of running down into an overshadowing bluff, with a steamboat—showing that my earliest dread made the strongest impression on me (running steadily down the deep shadows of Selma Bluffs & head of Hat Island" (no close parenthesis, *N&J2*, 450).

Mark Twain's notebook entries suggest that he often genuinely enjoyed this trip as a passenger. When the experience was translated into chapters 22–60 of *Life on the Mississippi,* however, it produced a cumulatively morbid, even frightening, impression. The book is in many respects unmonitored and constitutes a tainted stew, hastily assembled. As with *A Tramp Abroad,* Twain underestimated the number of pages he needed. He complained to his publisher, James R. Osgood, on September 18, 1882, of being "half dead with malaria," and "what is worse than all that is that I find I still lack about 30,000 words, whereas a few days ago I thought it was only a third of that—dismal miscalculation!" (*MTLP*, 157–58). To fill up the vacancy, he shoveled in a variety of materials, including the "Raftsmen's Passage" from *Huckleberry Finn,* leftover parts of the *Tramp,* and long citations from various local histories and travel books.[1] He reported to Howells late in October: "Result of the day: (mainly stolen from books, tho' credit given,) 9500 words . . . I have nothing more to borrow or steal; the rest must all be writing" (*MTHL* 1:417). In the next letter he was complaining of having "the burden of these unfilled gaps harassing me and the thought of the broken continuity of the work, while I am at the same time trying to build build [*sic*] the last quarter of the book" (*MTHL* 1:418). By January 15, 1883, he had overshot the mark and was telling Osgood that he had added "footnotes and other stuff . . . I put in some Southern assassinations." He now estimated that he had "20 to 25,000 more words than necessary; so the scissors can be freely used. The whole family sick, here" (*MTLP,* 162). The scissors, if used, were used inexpertly. The last four chapters devoted to the trip by boat north from St. Louis to St. Paul are particularly uneven, composed of anecdotes loosely connected to the narrative at best, long excerpts from Henry Rowe Schoolcraft's Indian legends, and flat statistical observations such as this: "Opposite Davenport is the flourishing town of Rock Island, which lies at the foot of the Upper Rapids. A great railroad bridge connects the two towns—one of the thirteen which fret the Mississippi and the pilots between St. Louis and St. Paul" (336).

The assembling of *Life on the Mississippi* was then an exasperating experience for Mark Twain. "I never had such a fight over a book in my life before" (*MTHL* 1:418). Although such exasperation as well as family problems may have had their effect, the miasma of negativity that hangs

1. Walter Blair, *Mark Twain and Huck Finn* (Berkeley, 1962), 289; 410, fn. 7. See also the detailed genetic study, Horst H. Kruse, *Mark Twain and "Life on the Mississippi"* (Amherst, Mass., 1981), 93–124.

over the bulk of the book was deepened by a series of dis-illusionments encountered on what he called "this hideous trip" (*MTL,* 2:419). They included hearing the fates of pilots he had known twenty years earlier on the river; observing destructive shifts of the river's course and the degradation of familiar towns; having his prejudices about the South reinforced; and, most disillusioning of all, returning to the Hannibal of his youth. As he wrote Livy: "That world which I knew in its blossoming youth is old and bowed and melancholy, now. . . . I have been clasping hands with the moribund—and usually they said, 'It is for the last time'" (*MTL* 2:419).

Mark Twain was only forty-six when he wrote that, but this mood of late autumnal distress was sustained throughout the writing of the *Life.* It produced this aphorism: "The man who is a pessimist before he is forty-eight knows too much; the man who is an optimist after he is forty-eight knows too little" (*MTB,* 744). By the time he completed the book, that attitude so thoroughly permeated it that it might more accurately have been entitled "Death on the Mississippi."

Mark Twain's hardest task as a cub pilot had been to force himself to steer his boat directly into "a solid, straight wall" of darkness, trusting that it would fall back and make way for him (53). That imaginary bluff, which still produced nightmares, was associated with his profoundest fear—and guilt. "Solid blackness—a crackless bank of it"—generated unnerved terror in him, and although it was specifically associated with the river, it also went back to childhood fears (339). When Twain was a boy, the night after a companion had drowned, "a ferocious thunder-storm" struck, there was "inky blackness," then lightning, "then the solid darkness shut down again" (313). On this nostalgic trip, that black wall loomed over him, again and again.

Annihilation commenced as early as St. Louis. There he

perceived that the glory of steamboats "had dissolved and vanished away" (137). Now along the waterfront there was only "a wide and soundless vacancy," which struck him as "melancholy" and "woeful" (140). Although the city proper was progressing, "the river-edge of it seems dead past resurrection" (140). Mark Twain elected to think of the commercial changes here as murder and, moreover, as part of a Darwinian struggle. The steamboats had "killed" the keelboats, then were in their turn killed by the railroads and freight barges (141).

As he started down the river, Mark Twain anthropomorphized the steamboats of the past and their perils. Passing a shoal of sunken rocks, he observed that they were "admirably arranged to capture and kill steamboats on bad nights." Accordingly, "a good many steamboat corpses lie buried there" (152). Those corpses would be found through the rest of the book, sprawled, mutilated, and rotting. Nature was generally destructive. Familiar islands "were missing—washed away" (153). Floods caused "fearful" destruction of property (160). Now that the steamboat traffic had diminished, the huge indifference of the Mississippi itself awed Twain. "The loneliness of this solemn, stupendous flood is impressive—and depressing" (161). Reflecting on its "blank, watery solitude," he arrived at a cosmic desolation. In the following description, notice the gradual transition from divine magnificence to divine entropy. The Mississippi, Twain wrote, invariably presents the same monotonous face, "majestic, unchanging sameness of serenity, repose, tranquillity, lethargy, vacancy—symbol of eternity, realization of the heaven pictured by priest and prophet, and longed for by the good and thoughtless!" (161). The phrases after the dash reiterate the pattern of moving from the conventional to a helplessly nihilistic description.

The river carried fundamental feelings of despair for Mark Twain. If one asks why he left the river to go to Nevada, one must once more consider the intolerable demands that the river put on Twain's memory, the nightmarish solid walls of blackness, the shifting and deceptive fluid surfaces, the hidden reefs and snags, and the raw evidence of natural savagery associated with the river, for all these counteract and overwhelm Mark Twain's boyish romanticism that was initially hypnotized by the idea of being the man in complete control on the bridge, the man whom others obeyed without question or delay, the object of young women's and children's adoration. One can see the process of dread overcoming the pride of position when Twain recounts his discovery that four out of five of his former pilot friends had become farmers. Why? Because farming was an isolated occupation "like the pilot-house hermitage" but also, and more profoundly meaningful for the apprehensive Twain, "because on a thousand nights of black storm and danger they had noted the twinkling lights of solitary farmhouses . . . and pictured to themselves the serenity and security and coziness of such refuges" (283).

On this trip, then, the river was the focus of destructiveness for Mark Twain. More often than not, each place he passed or visited offered a new tale of horror. Fort Pillow? It was "memorable because of the massacre perpetrated there during the war" (173).[2] Island 37? Because it was purportedly where John Murel's gang stayed, it inspired several pages of quotations from an account of the

2. The Fort Pillow Massacre followed an attack by Confederate forces under General Nathan Bedford Forrest. After the fort, largely manned by black soldiers, was overrun, it was alleged that the prisoners were vindictively slaughtered. The issue is still under dispute; the massacre was probably not so thorough as suggested in the initial public outcry in the North, but on the other hand, numerous unarmed men *were* murdered. Both the horror and its ambiguities lie behind Mark Twain's mere reference to Fort Pillow.

gang's activities, which provided not only filler but also grisly details. If Murel did not inspire the respect that Slade had in *Roughing It,* he was equally merciless. "I shot him through the back of the head. I ripped open his belly, and took out his entrails and sunk him in the creek" (176). Memphis? "A beautiful city, nobly situated," but a description of a yellow fever epidemic takes precedence in Twain's account (178). All of these details appear in a chapter entitled "A Few Specimen Bricks," a title never explicitly referred to in the text but one that certainly suggests the nature of the edifice Twain was examining. These were bricks of misery.

The pervasive mood of mutilation and horror expands in specific stories. In the *Tramp,* Twain had collected legends that involved the inadvertent destruction of a loved one. He continues that disconcerting practice in the *Life.* Here it is one "Captain Poe" whose boat had struck a snag and who, in his attempt to rescue his wife, took an axe to the deck forming the ceiling of his wife's stateroom—"and clove her skull" (185).[3] It is all very improbable, but putting aside the psychological continuity of mistakenly killing loved ones, the grisliness itself is consonant with the gruesome aura of this Mississippi trip. Later, reporting the memories of a participant in the siege of Vicksburg, Twain offers another implausible anecdote in which as a man is shaking the hand of a friend, an artillery shell "cut the man's arm off, and left it dangling in my hand" (206).

This general atmosphere of Grand Guignol encouraged Mark Twain to add a particularly unpleasant reminiscence of an encounter he ostensibly had had in Munich the previous

3. In Poe's "The Black Cat," the narrator, enraged by his wife's interference, turns on her "and buried the axe in her brain" (*Collected Works of Edgar Allan Poe,* ed. Thomas O. Mabbott [Cambridge, Mass., 1978], 3:856).

year with a dying man who had worked as night watchman in the morgue (or "dead-house" or "corpse-room") (196). The man tells a story of seeking revenge on two other men who had murdered his wife and daughter. The aggrieved husband and father found the morgue a hospitable place. "I liked it. I liked being with the dead—liked being alone with them. I used to wander among those rigid corpses, and peer into their austere faces, by the hour" (196).

Imaginatively, that approximates what Mark Twain was doing on this journey. In its most distressing manifestations, Twain's language tells us how grotesque such contemplation could be. Just below Hannibal was a cave. In it was the body of a fourteen-year-old girl, enclosed in a "copper cylinder filled with alcohol." Since the top was removable, "it was said to be a common thing for the baser order of tourists to drag the dead face into view and examine it and comment upon it" (324). Twain said he would have liked to revisit the cave but had not the time. Nonetheless, he was doing precisely this, metaphorically—dragging death into the light, looking it in the face, and commenting upon it.

When Mark Twain needed additional material, he provided a footnote of some sixty lines intended as an ironic account of a college prospectus asserting that the South represented the acme of American civilization. As "illustrations . . . thoughtlessly omitted by the advertisers," Twain included detailed newspaper accounts of four violent incidents involving shotguns ("found him playing billiards in a saloon, and blew his brains out"), clubs, axes, and butcher knives (239, 241). Further, when he arrived in New Orleans, his attention rapidly focused on its burial practices. Because the city was built on landfill, its citizens "bury their dead in vaults, above the ground" (247). Although initially complimentary about the excellent maintenance of these cemeteries, Twain suddenly pronounced their very existence anathema: they were "grotesque, ghastly, horrible" (248). He then launched, unexpectedly and with an intensity that takes one aback, an attack on the burial of bodies as opposed to their cremation. Bodies, he wrote, "glut the earth, the plant-roots, and the air with disease-germs," causing many deaths (248). Moreover, funerals were an unnecessary financial expense. Then as if becoming aware of the personal intensity of his argument, Twain begins a new chapter, "The Art of Inhumation." In it, he invents a dialogue between himself and an undertaker who enthusiastically explains how money is to be made in the business. Epidemics, the undertaker says, are not, as one might suppose, good for business, because the two items that are the most profitable for undertakers—ice and embalming—are not wanted: "Well, don't you see, when there's an epidemic, people don't wait to embam [*sic*]" (254). In an epidemic, people are anxious to bury their dead swiftly.

Mark Twain was always preoccupied with corpses. There is the grave robbing and the cannon firing to make drowned corpses rise in *Tom Sawyer;* Pap dead in the wrecked house on the river, and Boggs, and Buck Grangerford in *Huckleberry Finn:* the corpse in his father's office; and his memory of having seen an autopsy performed on his father.[4] The power of the dead was an idea susceptible to a richly creative transformation in the *Life* when he drew on the "raftsmen passage" originally composed for *Huckleberry Finn* but omitted when that book appeared to be running too long (*N&J*3, 98, fn. 104). He inserted it at the beginning of the *Life* "by way of illustrating keelboat talk and man-

---

4. For the autopsy on his father, whose identity Twain displaced—"Witnessed post mortem of my uncle through the keyhole"—see Dixon Wecter, *Sam Clemens of Hannibal* (Boston, 1952), 116.

ners, and that now departed and hardly remembered raft life" (16).

The episode has often been discussed because of its powerfully observed sketch of river life and talk. But more significant for this discussion—for the underlying mood of *Life on the Mississippi* and, even more deeply, for Mark Twain's conception of himself as a writer and public figure—is the latter part of the passage. Huck surreptitiously boards a large raft and listens to its crew, joking, boasting, telling stories. Then the muddiness of the Mississippi water brings forth the joke that those who drink it provide an unusually good fertilizer when they die, compared with someone brought up on, say, Ohio water. "A Cincinnati corpse don't richen a soil any" (20). That association leads to ghosts, which then take the group to the main story. It concerns a raftsman who had once inadvertently choked his child to death when it was crying and had buried it in a barrel. Thereafter that barrel floats near any raft he is working on. When it is finally brought on board and opened, he admits his crime and, seizing the baby's body, jumps into the river and disappears.

The story doesn't impress the raftsmen. They ask impertinent but realistic questions, such as "how could it *keep* all that time?" (25). But Huck has absorbed the story, so that when he is later discovered on the raft and asked his name, he blurts out the name of the dead baby—"Charles William Allbright, sir" (26). The relation of the names here is intricate, but not without meaning. "Allbright" is itself ironic, given the world Huck, the baby, and Mark Twain know. Further, though, Huck is specifically identified in this episode as "nothing but a cub"; Mark Twain himself would shortly be presented as a cub in the *Life's* narrative, since the raftsmen's passage is placed before his adventures as an apprentice pilot. More. Later in the *Life* Twain tells a story of a burglar-confidence man, son of a New England clergyman and graduate of Harvard, who concocted a letter when he was in prison, which was ostensibly by a fellow convict now released. After supposedly attributing his salvation to the burglar's Christian efforts, this fellow convict ended the bogus letter by expressing the fear that the burglar might die of consumption in prison. (See *N&J*2, 508.) The letter, intended to secure the release of the prisoner, moved a series of clergymen and their congregations to tears but was ultimately revealed as an imposture, written by the prisoner himself. His name was "Charles Williams." As the prison chaplain wrote, "Charles Williams is not a Christian man, but a dissolute, cunning prodigal" (305). So, from society's point of view, was Huck, who temporarily assumed the name "Charles William Allbright." So was Mark Twain.

Pseudonyms are everywhere in Mark Twain's work and life. On this very trip, he assumed a fictitious name but reported that he had difficulty remembering it (135).[5] Later in the *Life* he told how he had won what he calls his "nom de guerre" (291). The account is psychologically peculiar. Twain recalls a famous patriarchal figure among riverboat pilots, one Isaiah Sellers. Sellers knew the river intimately and occasionally published "paragraphs of plain, practical information about the river" that he would supposedly sign "Mark Twain." Although the pilots were impressed by Sellers's professional knowledge, the personal interjections he added to his paragraphs were the object of their derision. Therefore, when he was a cub, Mark Twain undertook to burlesque the style of Sellers's paragraphs. His mockery, he said, hurt Sellers so deeply that the master pilot "did me

5. The name Clemens used has been rendered in three different versions: "C. L. Samuels" (*N&J*2, 486, n. 73); "S. L. Samuel" (*MTHL* 1:401); and "C. L. Samuel" (*MTL,* 2:417). Whatever the actual choice, Clemens was obviously reversing his own name.

the honor to profoundly detest me from that day forth" (291). Furthermore, Twain's irreverence in effect permamently silenced the older man. "He never printed another paragraph while he lived, and he never again signed 'Mark Twain' to anything." Accordingly, when Clemens needed a pseudonym "on the Pacific coast," he said he "confiscated" this one (291). In a letter to Osgood he said, "I stole my nom de plume from him" (*MTLP*, 157).

If ever there was a case of symbolic patricide, this was it. Mark Twain imaginatively won his pseudonym by conquest.[6] At the same time, one recalls that in the "Old Times" section, "Mark twain" was the cry associated with terrible dangers and embarrassments for its owner. Pseudonyms in Mark Twain's work signify his awareness of the multiplicity of his identities. The pseudonyms emerge out of an intuitive sense of their rightness. "Charles William Allbright" contains associations of abuse, irony, and fate. "Charles Williams" suggests fraudulence in writing that was composed to escape from a prison. "Mark Twain" signifies personal disaster but also the victory of a younger man over a knowledgeable but tedious master.

Mark Twain's return to Hannibal was meant to constitute a triumph, but his immersion in boyhood memories took a disconcerting turn. Twain was struck at once by the contrast between the town's setting and its inhabitants. He thought the view at Hannibal "very beautiful" still. It seemed altogether "young and fresh and comely and gracious," whereas the faces of the people he met were "old,

---

6. The background to Twain's sketch and the sketch itself as well as a suggestion that Sellers had once struck Clemens in the nose with a boot appears in *ET&S*1, 126–33. On the other hand, Sellers may never have actually used the name "Mark Twain." For my purposes it is sufficient that Mark Twain *claimed* this was Sellers's pseudonym and that he appropriated it as a right of conquest.

and scarred with the campaigns of life, and marked with their griefs and defeats" (308). This contrast was then succeeded by a conversation with an old gentleman whom Mark Twain asked about several old acquaintances. Out of a dozen or so specific people, only three had turned out prosperously, and one of these falls into the equivocal category of ironic success, since this person, now the "first lawyer" of Missouri, had been "a perfect chucklehead" as a boy, a "perfect dummy; just a stupid ass" (310). As to the others, although they were promising as children, their fates were notably disappointing. The first two graduated with honors from Eastern colleges, but one was "supposed to have gone to the dogs," the other "died in one of the territories, years ago, a defeated man" (309). Another studied a profession, married, drank, gambled, abandoned his family, went off to Mexico, "and finally died there, without a cent to buy a shroud." Yet Mark Twain remembered him as having been "the best-natured and most cheery and hopeful young fellow that ever was" (309). One of Twain's early sweethearts was "all right," but had been "married three times; buried two husbands, divorced from the third." Yet another young woman "died in the insane asylum" (309, 310).

The general impression given of Hannibal is of a preponderant unhappiness. When misery struck, Mark Twain included details, whereas when things turned out all right, his description was laconic. "Oh, he is all right. Lives here yet; has a wife and children, and is prospering" (309). Success did not always please him. Resentment and contempt for conventional behavior are directed against "the Model Boy . . . admiration of all the mothers, and the detestation of all their sons." In learning his fate as an adult—"he succeeded in life"—Twain admits to "disappointment" (319).

Following the list of former acquaintances and their subsequent careers, Mark Twain launched a series of extended anecdotes, all having to do with disaster. Two boys drowned, one of whom, "Dutchy," was entangled under water where he died. Twain, according to his story, was obliged to dive down in the muddy water to see what had happened and "presently grasped a limp wrist which gave no response" (317). The pickled daughter in the copper cylinder also appears at this point, as does the "harmless, whisky-sodden tramp" to whom Twain gave the matches with which the tramp subsequently burned himself to death (325).

Hannibal essentially represented sudden death in such catastrophes or slow death in the disappointments suffered by adults. During the three days of his visit, Twain said he woke each morning feeling like a boy, for in his dreams "the faces were all young again," but "I went to bed a hundred years old, every night, for meantime I had been seeing those faces as they are now" (320). This mood continued through the next decade. By early 1891, Twain's vision was totally overcast. "Tom comes, at last, 60 from wandering the world & tends Huck, & together they talk the old times; both are desolate, life has been a failure, all that was lovable, all that was beautiful is under the mould. They die together" (*N&J*3, 606).

Even if Mark Twain had not been congenitally disposed to look apprehensively on existence, his experience on the trip and during the composition of the *Life* would have encouraged uneasiness. The steamboat *Gold Dust,* on which he had traveled from St. Louis to Vicksburg, blew up a few months later, killing seventeen, including the pilot (226). Meanwhile, Twain's house was put under quarantine as first Jean and then, apparently, Susy went down with scarlet fever (*N&J*2, 435; *MTHL* 1:406, 408). No wonder that much of the balance of the journey failed to inspire him. Consider his summary: "From St. Louis northward there are all the enlivening signs of the presence of active, energetic, intelligent, prosperous, practical nineteenth-century populations. [Had Twain meant this assessment, he would have put an "and" between each adjective, for he invariably separated qualities he wished to emphasize and savor.] The people don't dream; they work. The happy result is manifest all around in the substantial outside aspect of things, and the suggestions of wholesome life and comfort that everywhere appear" (330). But wholesome comfort was not what interested Twain. He was past the superficial but affectionate satire of *Tom Sawyer* and moving deeper into the dangerous world of Huck Finn. So the last four chapters of the *Life* are shallow and perfunctory, save for a little stirring of Twain's imagination when he encounters some of Schoolcraft's Indian legends.

One of these, "The Undying Head," he characterizes as containing "weird conceits" and "fairy-tale prodigies," but since it was "a rather long tale," he relegates it to Appendix D, where it effectively concludes *Life on the Mississippi* (346). The story is a bizarre one, guaranteed to attract Twain's attention, for it involves disaster brought on by a woman, decapitation, repeated melodramatic threats, and finally an ambiguously happy ending.

All the details of the story (which was not created but selected by Mark Twain) are not necessary to know. Its main relationship is that of an adult male Indian and his sister who are living alone together. When she comes to maturity, the brother tells her: "Sister, the time is at hand when you will be ill. Listen to my advice. If you do not, it will probably be the cause of my death" (372). Given his insistence that she live apart when she is ill, the illness would appear to be the initial onset of menstruation. In his commentary, Schoolcraft elaborates: "Nothing is better attested, by those who have given attention to this subject, than that everything touched by the female during this period is polluted and rendered unclean."[7] By mistake, the sister fails to obey her brother, whereupon, saying "You have killed me," he begins to turn black from the feet up (372). He then instructs her to cut off his head, put it in an open-ended sack, and hang it up in the lodge, which she does. Henceforth, the head guides her actions from its sack. After all parties endure much suffering, the head solves all the problems and is at last rejoined to its body. At the end of the story, the brother and sister "descended into the depths below," a conclusion that is presumably meant as satisfactory, even though the imagery of descending into depths, associated as it is with death and the underworld, markedly qualifies our feelings of gratification (382).[8]

On that ambiguous note, *Life on the Mississippi* ends. The book is an exceedingly uneven performance, broken backed, evasive, patchy, but with some extraordinary segments in it. Most remarkable is its demonstration of Mark Twain's reflecting first on his apprenticeship and then moving even further back into his youth, releasing memories of humiliation and terror. The sense he revivified in writing the *Life* of the anarchic dangers of the world, of men's untrustworthiness, and of his own uncertain role in this threatening environment carried over into the middle reaches of *Huckleberry Finn*. Although the trip down the river had made him a boy again, this boy was no longer the con-

7. Henry Rowe Schoolcraft, *Algic Researches* (New York, 1839), 1:121.

8. In "The Appendix of *Life on the Mississippi*," Richard Lettis argues that the four appendices represent a coherent body of advice on approaching a force as dangerous as the river. "The Undying Head," in particular, "celebrates the power of seeing and dealing with that which threatens man" (*Mark Twain Journal* 21, no. 2 [Summer 1982], 12).

fident, comfortable fantasist Tom but the homeless indigent Huck, on the run from a world that gave him nightmares at night and then embodied them by day in a sordid and frightening reality. Writing the *Life* had been less a trip down the Mississippi than one down into Twain's psyche.

7

Mark Twain composed *Following the Equator* under at least double duress. Although the demands of business forced him to make twelve Atlantic crossings in four years (1891–1895), he had no intention of writing another travel book until a cluster of financial problems drove him into bankruptcy in 1894. Then after making an arduous lecture trip around the world, he had just settled in England to construct a money-making book when a cable arrived announcing the death of his favorite daughter Susy on August 18, 1896. He did not begin the book for another two months. Finally on October 24, 1896, he made this entry in his notebook: "Wrote the first chapter of the book today—*Around the World*" (*MTB,* 1026).

The combination of giving lectures on the international tour and recounting his reactions to the trip in a book was intended to regain him solvency. As he said in a well-known interview with the *New York Times* as he embarked on the voyage: "I am confident that, if I live I can pay off the last debt within four years, after which, at the age of sixty-four, I can make a fresh and unincumbered start in life." But he added: "I do not enjoy the hard travel and broken rest inseparable from lecturing, and, if it had not been for the imperious moral necessity of paying these debts . . . I should never have taken to the road at my time of life" (*MTHHR,* 182).

He was in fact fifty-nine when the trip commenced and in indifferent health. He was especially cursed with car-

buncles. "I'll go to Cleveland in a stretcher, sure," he observed shortly before he was to start (*MTHHR,* 158). Six
months later, on board ship, approaching Ceylon, he again
wrote: "I have been persecuted with carbuncles and colds
until I am tired and disgusted and angry" (*MTHHR,* 190).
At that point the trip still had six months to go. A. B. Paine
reports that "the papers usually spoke of him as looking
frail," and his wife wrote that "Mr. Clemens has not as
much courage as I wish he had," a lack she attributed not
only to his illnesses but also to his being "so impressed
with the fact that he is sixty years old." Moreover, their
bankruptcy understandably weighed on him. "He does not
believe that any good thing will come, but that we must all
our lives live in poverty. He says he never wants to go back
to America" (*MTB,* 1017).

It would be difficult, then, to exaggerate the burden of
wretchedness that bore down on Mark Twain before he
undertook to write *Following the Equator:* it included debts,
aging, illness, fatigue, and Susy's death. At the same time,
he did enjoy much of the traveling. He had always taken
pleasure in being lionized, and the exotic countries he visited kept him stimulated. Not only was he a celebrity in his
own right, but his financial adviser, Henry Huttleston
Rogers of Standard Oil, assisted when he could in seeing
that Clemens was properly cared for. "The government
railway treated us well," Clemens wrote from Calcutta.
"Private car and elegant food etc." (*MTHHR,* 195). So
Livy attested that "in spite of this sad undercurrent, we are
having a delightful trip" (*MTB,* 1017). These fluctuating
moods are visible in *Following the Equator,* although it must
be said that on the whole, as far as humor is concerned, it is
a flat and uninspired work.[1] But new and serious social and

1. *Following the Equator* has not been much commented on,
and reactions to it have been both vague and mixed. James Cox

philosophic issues were coming to the fore in Mark Twain's mind. Although he claimed that he had consciously written the book for the "subscription market," that is, for "the factory hands and the farmers," since he believed that the audience who shopped at bookstores were "surfeited with travel-books," the serious social arguments do not seem directed toward the subscription-book audience (*MTHHR,* 249–50). Mark Twain's harsh criticism of the whites for their exploitation of people of color was far from guaranteed to win rural and working-class approval.

If the overall tone of the *Equator* were not determinable from the text itself, its chapter epigraphs would furnish evidence enough of a new authorial grimness. The book *Pudd'nhead Wilson* had appeared in 1894. Since then Mark Twain had accumulated a fresh store of the lawyer's steely maxims, designated as from "Pudd'nhead Wilson's New Calendar." Powerful, mordant, pessimistic, cynical, they now headed the *Equator's* chapters and dealt with the untrustworthiness of friends, the criminality of legislative representatives and of lawyers, the contradictoriness of man's nature, the pathos of life, and the desirability of death. In short, they capture Twain's increasing nihilism, a nihilism to which he was yielding in spite of an often buoyant and compassionate nature. The severity of his vision was bringing him to succinct statements: "Pity is for the living, envy is for the dead" (184).

At times, the maxims fit the material that follows; more

---

calls it "that last, and interesting, travel book" (*The Fate of Humor* [Princeton, 1966], 245fn.). Kenneth Lynn says it is "a sorry affair, the only uninteresting travel book Twain ever wrote" (*Mark Twain and Southwestern Humor* [Boston, 1959], 277). And in mediation, William Gibson proposes that it is "a decidedly better book than all but a few critics have said in print" (*The Art of Mark Twain* [New York, 1976], 158–59).

often they stand independent of the journey's incidents, casting a pall across whatever humor Twain could generate. The issue of natural intention is addressed in the maxim for chapter thirty: "Nature makes the locust with an appetite for crops; man would have made him with an appetite for sand" (285). Similarly, while in New Zealand, Twain was shown a lignified caterpillar with a plant growing out of it as the result of fungal spores that had implanted themselves there. He again emphasizes that this was "by design—Nature's design" (288). As other examples of such malign intentionality, he adds the attraction of moths to candle flames, the invasion of a starfish by parasites, and the "unperfected tapeworm" (288–89).

This brief flurry of indignation at the cruel ways of Nature presumably emerged from the blows it had inflicted on him and his family, especially in the past year, although earlier his only son, Langdon, had contracted a fatal case of diphtheria and more recently his daughter Jean had been diagnosed as an epileptic, so that Twain might well have felt himself and all living things in the grip of a mighty and inexplicably malevolent force. This feeling may account for his fatalistic reaction to the party's arrival in Hawaii. It being night, the ship anchored off Honolulu. After an absence of more than thirty years, he was "impatient" to land. But when morning came, "it brought disappointment, of course": an outbreak of cholera that prevented their going ashore.

Proximity to Honolulu unsurprisingly reminded him then of lepers and their dreadful deformities. One in particular, like Twain's Hannibal acquaintances, was "a brilliant young fellow, and very popular," engaged to "a beautiful half-caste girl." (He was "a half-white"—success, advancement, leadership were still white; characteristically, seductiveness and submissiveness were "half-caste." This inadvertent bias would be tempered before the trip was over.)

The young man, having contracted leprosy, was obliged to give up his career and fiancée and go to isolation on Molokai, where "he died the loathsome and lingering death that all lepers die." Twain underlines that all "these poor sufferers are innocent" (63).

The whole trip, undertaken reluctantly, started unpropitiously. Mark Twain, suffering from his carbuncle, remarked that the dictionary defined it as "a kind of jewel," but that "humor was out of place in a dictionary" (25). Their departure was delayed because of a raging forest fire near Vancouver, and just as they got under way, their deck chairs collapsed, which "brought us to shame before all the passengers" (16). All of these misfortunes are treated humorously, but the signs were ominous.

The captain of their ship, although the acme of excellence—young, "very handsome," "courteous"—nonetheless "was going home under a cloud" (27–28). On his first trip in command, he had run his ship onto the rocks, and although apparently blameless and already officially exonerated by the admiralty court, he still had to face the economic wrath of the shipowners back in Sydney. Later in the book Mark Twain inveighed against commercial shipowners for placing profits above human life. It was a subject about which he was unusually sensitive. One shipping company in particular "had discharged a captain for getting a boat into danger and had advertised this act as evidence of its vigilance in looking after the safety of the passengers." Twain, though, believed that the captain was no more than an expedient sacrifice—"thugging a captain costs a company nothing" (302).

His indignation was repeatedly ignited at the sacrifice of people to commercial gain. The New Zealand shipping company was "powerful," "it has a monopoly, and everybody is afraid of it—including the government's representative" (301). The experience, Twain thought, "was like being at home in America" (302). Later on, passing the Great Barrier Reef, Twain offered an almost identical indictment, recalling that a ship had struck the reef going "full-speed in a fog," with the loss of one hundred and forty lives. The captain immediately committed suicide, knowing "whether he was to blame or not, the company owning the vessel would discharge him and make a devotion-to-passengers'-safety advertisement out of it, and his chance to make a livelihood would be permanently gone" (311).

This preoccupation with the amoral depredations of business, especially in concert with imperialistic expansion, would appear more and more often in Mark Twain's writings after this. His own disastrous experiences in trying to run a publishing company and in technological speculation had sensitized him to commercial practices. Ironically, Twain's hostility enlarged just when he had become the intimate of such conservative magnates as Andrew Carnegie and H. H. Rogers. But whatever his overall contradictory feelings about predatory businessmen, Twain perceived and openly spoke out as a compassionate observer against inhumane and hypocritical social practices.

The young captain also gained Mark Twain's sympathy, one may suppose, because he had struck the rocks when his "narrow and difficult passage" had been "densely befogged with smoke"—precisely the nightmarish black wall Twain had always feared on the river (28). So too the harbor at Sydney, Australia, featured a precipice "like a wall" with but a single unobtrusive entrance through it (110). In his telling of the wreck of the *Duncan Dunbar* there, Twain not only emphasized the deceptiveness of the harbor entrance but also heightened the sentimental drama involved in the wreck there. He insisted that the ship "was bringing back a great company of mothers and daughters, the long-missed light and bloom of life of Sydney homes; daughters that had been years absent at school, and mothers that had been with them all that time watching over them" (111). That scenario may have been true, although it seems a little improbable, but one can readily understand how gripping the scene would be for this father of three daughters, one of whom had just died. The captain of the *Duncan Dunbar,* like Clemens pouring money into the Paige typesetter, "steered straight for the false opening, mistaking it for the true one. He did not find out that he was wrong until it was too late" (111).[2] Virtually unmonitored as much of this last travel book proved to be, Twain's storytelling in it often turns to private musing. This story and the special emphasis of its telling are clear examples of Mark Twain's drawing forth and shaping experience to entertain an audience, but also to achieve personal catharsis. Twain selected the story in the first place because he was preoccupied with piloting disasters; he heightened the special pain of the loss of "all that fair and gracious company" because he had recently lost his own daughter (111–12).

If the pathetic was in Mark Twain's soul during the writ-

2. Clemens's notebook entry reads: "It was dark & he mistook the false Heads for the real; struck, & his ship went to pieces like a box of matches." He also notes of the passengers: "They had their best clothes on & all. Sydney waiting for them—daughters educated in England, & well-to-do people returning from a holiday" (Notebook no. 38 [May–July 1896], *MTP*). The *Duncan Dunbar* carried sixty-three passengers and a crew of fifty-nine; only one of the latter survived. A recent account of the disaster does not refer to any special concentration of women and children among the passengers, but it does insist, in contradiction of Twain, that "the captain had not mistaken The Gap for the Harbour entrance . . . he had miscalculated his leeway" (P. R. Stephensen, *The History and Description of Sydney Harbour* [Adelaide, 1966], 28). For a contemporary newspaper account of the wreck, see *The Sydney Scene, 1788–1960,* arranged and introduced by Alan Birch and David S. Macmillan (Melbourne, 1962), 150–52.

ing of the *Equator,* so was his sense of the lugubrious. The "Sweet Singer of Michigan," Julia Moore, enters the book three times with her doggerel mourning (108, 325, 406). Given his own loss, it seems grotesque for Twain to quote her as he does. Here, for example, is her tribute to an only son who died while away from home (as Susy had died while the Clemenses were across the Atlantic): "He was taken sick and lived four weeks, / And Oh! how his parents weep, / But now they must in sorrow mourn, / For Billy has gone to his heavenly home" (325).

Twain himself attempted elegies for Susy on the anniversary of her death in 1897, 1898, and 1902.[3] Psychologically, it would seem that he occasionally had to mock the very grief that seized his household through the person of Julia Moore. Generally speaking, though, signs of unmitigated and even invented pessimism permeated the book. In recounting a shuffleboard tournament on shipboard, for example, Twain said that he had lost, whereas in a letter to Rogers, he reported that he had won (70–72; *MTHHR,* 187). So too when he viewed the Southern Cross, it seemed to him "out of repair," "out of true," but insofar as he could imagine it constituting a shape, it struck him as "a sort of coffin" (79). When the passengers engaged in a competition to provide an incomplete story with a happy ending, no one, including Twain himself, could do so (47). Reflecting on another story told of "two strange and solitary beings" who were picked up at sea, Twain was reminded of all those "errant waifs who cannot name their lost home, wandering Children of No-where." The very idea stimulated him to ponder the "island wilderness of the Pacific." It was a region, he said, with particular charm "for the bruised spirit of men who have fought and failed in the

---

3. See Arthur L. Scott, *On the Poetry of Mark Twain with Selections from His Verse* (Urbana, Ill., 1966), 30–32.

struggle for life in the great world" (99–100). As early as the tenth chapter, Pudd'nhead Wilson is quoted as saying: "Everything human is pathetic." Furthermore, Twain succinctly specified the wellspring of his art: "The secret source of Humor itself is not joy but sorrow. There is no humor in heaven" (119).

One way Mark Twain coped with the world's horror was to stare directly at it. One cannot altogether attribute the suffering, violence, and morbidity in *Following the Equator,* or in Twain's other works, to Twain himself; a measure of such horrors was integral to the age. As an example, in the text Twain remarks of the moa bird of New Zealand (which even then was extinct): "The Moa stood thirteen feet high, and could step over an ordinary man's head or kick his hat off; and his head too, for that matter" (102). The illustration shows an aborigine riding on a moa. Both he and the bird are looking back to where the great ostrich-like foot is kicking the head off a white man while blood spouts copiously from his neck.[4] Even if the illustration augmented Twain's remark, the audience was presumably not offended by the gratuitous gore.

Early on, Mark Twain reports the story of a professional diver who descended to a sunken passenger ship where he was "paralyzed with fright" from seeing numerous "dim corpses making for him" (57). As in Twain's earlier travel volumes we are also treated to extended descriptions of criminal violence, sometimes not even composed by Twain but merely inserted from newspapers or books. In New Zealand he revives the "Maungatapu Murders" of thirty

4. *Following the Equator* used eleven illustrators as well as photographs. Dan Beard did this full-page illustration of the moa, and as in *A Connecticut Yankee in King Arthur's Court,* the job afforded him an opportunity to punish the ruling class, for the decapitated white man is wearing a pith helmet, a monocle, and spats.

years earlier, producing explicit descriptions of strangling, shooting, and stabbing (305–7). In India, two chapters' worth of detailed attention is devoted to the practice of ritualistic murder. Twain speculated that the reason the Thugs killed was "partly piety, largely gain," but he thought the chief fascination of killing for them was the *"sport"* of it (436). This idea gave rise to a much more damning proposition: "The joy of killing! the joy of seeing killing done—these are the traits of the human race at large" (437). And in fact, probably not consciously, Twain was pandering to exactly those preoccupations in the *Equator.* He pushed the point further. "We white people are merely modified Thugs; Thugs fretting under the restraints of a not very thick skin of civilization" (437). As evidence, he adduced the spectacles of the Roman Colosseum, the burning of Christians by the Inquisition (he had just published *Joan of Arc*), the Spanish bullfight, and rabbit hunting. He paused for a moment to reflect that some progress had been made—"we no longer take pleasure in slaughtering or burning helpless men"—but then he plunged back into his description of the deceptiveness and murderousness of the Thugs (437).

The account of a prisoner in the Black Hole of Calcutta is also quoted at length. The prisoner's experience, which involved strenuous but civilized efforts to survive, was inspirational in its own way, since although eventually he fell unconscious, he was nonetheless saved. Perhaps Mark Twain too would in time be spared further suffering and would undergo a similar "resurrection from this hole of sorrows" (522). Among other reasons, we tell stories for comfort.

The famous "Great Mutiny" among the native garrisons of India again provided Twain with ample gruesome and pathetic stories, often quoted directly from contemporary sources. Men are beaten into the mud with cudgels, infants are torn to pieces, ladies' apartments are discovered "ankle-deep in blood," bodies are stripped and flung into dry wells (554–55). It is curious that following these horrible scenes of the Black Hole and the Great Mutiny, Twain should pass with no more transition than paragraphing to the most commonplace enumeration of tourist sights. "There was plenty to see in Calcutta, but there was not plenty of time for it. I saw the fort that Clive built; and the place where Warren Hastings and the author of the Junius Letters fought their duel; and . . ." (522). Such flat enumerations appear to serve as emotional calmatives, as decompression chambers following extended exposure to the pressures of human cruelty.

The overwhelming evidence Twain accumulated in the *Equator* that the innocent suffer inevitably raised the question *why*. Cast in the terms available to Mark Twain, the question concerned God's intention or, even more centrally, God's nature. Twain addressed the problem indirectly, in the voice of others, in fact at two discreet removes. To compare Hindu gods with the Christian one, Twain employs the voice of a missionary who in turn is reporting the argument of "a good old Hindoo gentleman" (133). The Hindu says that Christianity has not made greater inroads in the East because Indians "recognize a god by the work of his hands." Therefore one determines which gods are the stronger "by comparing the known works of his own gods with the works of others; there is no other way" (133). By this pragmatic test, the Hindus have found their deities much superior to the Christian God.

This is a devastating conclusion—so much so that Mark Twain was unwilling to take direct responsibility for it, however much he might believe it. He was always skittish about directly addressing religious issues in public. But the year after the *Equator* was published, he began to develop his ruminations on the matter extensively. They would finally appear anonymously as *What Is Man?*, published in

1906 in an edition limited to 250 copies that were not put on sale. Twain's ideas were already simmering as he prepared the *Equator,* although he thought that he had successfully concealed their presence. In an extraordinary letter to Howells, dated April 2, 1899, he said: "I wrote my last travel-book in hell; but I let on, the best I could, that it was an excursion through heaven. Some day I will read it, & if its lying cheerfulness fools me, then I shall believe it fooled the reader. How I did loathe that journey round the world!— except the sea-part & India" (*MTHL* 2:690).

As we've already seen, Mark Twain *had* been in distress while writing the *Equator,* and no doubt it had been a strain for him to maintain the humorous mask. Since the book contains a generous measure of suffering and indignation, though, it can hardly be said to exist in an unchanging climate of "lying cheerfulness." Rather, as was normal for Twain, he exhibited extreme fluctuations of mood, drifting in a sea of fundamental optimism at one moment, drowning in embittered cynicism at another. Such manifestations of extremes may bear upon the book's title. As was usually the case for him, the title came hard. In fact, the book ultimately appeared under two titles, for in England it was published as *More Tramps Abroad.* Before selecting that name, Twain had cast about in an uninspired way, trying out variants of his first great success: "Another Innocent Abroad," "An Old Innocence Abroad" (*MTHHR,* 275). He also considered "Imitating the Equator," saying that its meaning would be that "the equator goes around the world" (*MTHHR,* 269). Some versions of that must have been in his mind with the American title, *Following the Equator,* but its meaning is not immediately evident, especially since Twain's literal path, although crossing the equator several times, tends to follow the tropics of Cancer and Capricorn. The title also has two submerged meanings, however. To follow or imitate the equator was to adhere to a middle course, to avoid the polar extremes. It also meant coming around again to where one had started, in Twain's case, to Southampton, England, a conclusion that was at once reassuring in its symmetry and frustrating in its lack of progress.

Mark Twain's disgust with the ultimate absurdity of human life was pressing hard within him in 1899: "Since I wrote my Bible (last year) which Mrs. Clemens loathes, & shudders over, & will not listen to the last half nor allow me to print any part of it, Man is not to me the respect-worthy person he was before; & so I have lost my pride in him." Still, he avowed he would not try to publish his ideas. "For I don't wish to be scalped, any more than another" (*MTHL* 2:689). Nonetheless, he regarded humans as "God's beloved vermin," "the nasty, stinking little human race," "a poor joke—the poorest that was ever contrived—an April-fool joke, played by a malicious Creator with nothing better to waste his time upon" (*MTHL* 2:692, 689).

Mark Twain could never have proposed directly this contemptuous characterization of man and his God in a book for which he had crucial commercial aspirations. Still, the pressure of such ideas in his mind made an impress on *Following the Equator*. Back when he had been in his middle thirties and was contemplating the fraudulences of the Holy Land in *The Innocents Abroad,* he was still operating largely in a Christian context. In Asia, though, whole new cosmic systems appeared, believed in by millions of people. So Pudd'nhead Wilson now offered a definition of faith as "believing what you know ain't so" (132).

During his journey through India, Mark Twain encountered two living gods. The claim that he had nicknamed his servant "Satan" permitted this incongruous exchange when the servant appeared. "What is it, Satan?" "God want to see you." "*Who?*" "God. I show him up, master?" (366). The first of these gods living on earth, the object of the devotion of "multitudinous followers," magnetized Twain's attention. "I was looking upon a *god,* an actual god, a recognized and accepted god; and every detail of his person and dress had a consuming interest for me" (366–67). As it turned out, the "Awful Visitor" came to discuss "a feature of the philosophy of Huck Finn" (367).

Impressed by the exalted level of his readership, Twain in Benares *presented* the second living god he met with a copy of *Huckleberry Finn.* The act is described with a faint edge of facetiousness, yet Twain clearly meant it when he said, "I knew that if it didn't do him any good it wouldn't do him any harm" (512). He was not only consorting with gods; he could even think of enlightening them. Reflecting on the encounter, he initiated the problematic but undeveloped argument that we revere only things integral to our own culture—"parents, religion, flag, laws." These, he said, involve "feelings which we cannot even help." But he doubted the reality of fundamental belief: "Deep down in our hearts we are all irreverent" (514).

As this line of thought was broaching dangerous areas, its implications were left unexamined. Mark Twain himself was not a man without reverential feelings, however much he scoffed, but he could not locate a subject permanently worthy of his devotion, except perhaps, like Huck, certain scenes of natural beauty, and of suffering innocence. For example, he reflected at length on the custom of suttee in which the Indian widow voluntarily cremated herself on her husband's funeral pyre. At first Twain supposed that it must be public opinion that drives the widow to such an unnatural act, but he then was presented with an instance in which, after suttee had been outlawed in a district, a widow insisted on immolating herself against all entreaties. Twain concluded: "It is fine and beautiful. It compels one's reverence and respect—no, has it freely, and without compulsion" (456).

Mark Twain also contemplated the Parsee "Towers of Silence," where corpses were exposed to the vultures, and the Hindu cremation-ghat, where corpses were burned. But no consoling truths came forth at either place, only revulsion and mystery (371–77, 500–502). He was constantly driven back into life, which, if anything, became all the more enigmatic. In the Darwinian universe, the duckbilled platypus is proposed as the prime example of survival of the fittest. Twain's account of it, being decidedly sacrilegious, was again put in the mouth of another, this time a young English naturalist not otherwise identified (100). "Ornithorhyncus" did not enter the Ark. "It nobly stayed out and worked the theory." As the "*e pluribus unum* of the natural world" the platypus is supremely adapted. "It is carnivorous, herbivorous, insectivorous, and vermifuginous." "It is clearly a bird, for it lays eggs and hatches them; it is clearly a mammal, for it nurses its young; and it is manifestly a kind of Christian, for it keeps the Sabbath when there is anybody around, and when there isn't, doesn't" (102–5). The grotesqueness of this creature successfully adapted to the rigorous variety of the world provides amusement to Mark Twain, but underlying his description is a sense of the farcical developments necessary to survive. The platypus offers Twain no more answer than the anomalous *Pteraspis* that refused to evolve offered Henry Adams.

Touched in throughout the *Equator* are other attempts to reach clarity about a satisfactory life. These involve color, sensuality, and sexuality. The tropical silks of Ceylon ravished Mark Twain. His page describing the native costumes is crossed with amazed gratitude. The panorama they created was "stunning," "exquisite," "harmonious," "splendid," "and made the heart sing for gladness" (340). When his daughter Clara was married in 1909, Clemens wore his scarlet Oxford gown (representing his honorary doctor of letters degree) over white flannels (*MTB*, 1524). It was that man who responded to the brilliant Ceylonese display with unreserved enthusiasm: it was "glowing, flashing, burning, radiant; and every five seconds came a burst of blinding red that made a body catch his breath, and filled his heart with joy" (340).

Then "into this dream of fairyland and paradise" Twain marched a band of Christian schoolgirls. Their clothing was "a grating dissonance . . . was unspeakably ugly! Ugly, barbarous, destitute of taste, destitute of grace, repulsive as a shroud" (343).

In these opposed responses, one of passionate celebration, the other of disapproving disgust, Mark Twain's sensual nature is visible as well as the mantle of repression that normally covered it. Behind his enthusiasm for "that radiant panorama . . . that incomparable dissolving-view of harmonious tints, and lithe half-covered forms" was, to be sure, sexuality, display conceived for physical attraction, but that was a subject Twain could barely approach (340–43). Later in the book he did focus on the worship in India of the lingam. At the commencement of creation, it had been "no larger than a stovepipe." Now, "priapus-worship" is found to be universal. The lingam was "on view everywhere, it is garlanded with flowers, offerings are made to it, it suffers no neglect" (480, 482). Just how this and other such references passed Livy's editorial pen is not clear, especially since in editing the manuscript of the *Equator,* she firmly declared: "Change Breech clout. It is a word that you love & I abominate. I would take that & offal out of the language. Also stink."[5] Perhaps the sheer volume of lingams overwhelmed her. So omnipresent were the phallic representations in Benares that Twain concluded the city might well have been named Lingamburg (504).

5. Cited in Paul J. Carter, "Olivia Clemens Edits *Following the Equator,*" *American Literature* 30, no. 2 (May 1958): 203. When

That, however, is as far as Mark Twain's flirtation with sexuality goes, except insofar as men are concerned. Here he manifested some interest combined with a slight uneasiness. In Ceylon his servant was a "gentle, smiling, winning young brown creature" with "beautiful shining black hair combed back like a woman's." Twain found him "and his outfit quite unmasculine," so that "it was an embarrassment to undress before him" (336–39).

A more ambiguous paragraph concerns the fruit of the durian, well known because although its rind gives off a dreadful odor, its flesh is delicious. Mark Twain's description begins in a peculiar way that may signal an underlying playfulness: "I wonder if the *dorian,* if that is the name of it, is another superstition" (478). He makes a point about the name of the fruit, including italicizing that name, even though the fruit is normally known as the "durian." On the other hand, Oscar Wilde had published *The Picture of Dorian Gray* in 1891, at which time it became the center of furious social censure because of its overt hedonism and because of the barely concealed bisexuality of the principal character. When Wilde sued the marquess of Queensberry in 1895 for criminal libel, the marquess having alleged that the book

---

A. B. Paine quoted this passage in *MTB,* he dropped "Also stink" (1040). On the whole, Carter finds Livy less prudish than usually supposed. His evidence has been amplified by Sydney J. Krause in "Olivia Clemens's 'Editing' Reviewed," *American Literature* 39, no. 3 (November 1967): 325–51. In his 1974 New York University dissertation, "Mark Twain's Passage to India: A Genetic Study of *Following the Equator,*" Francis V. Madigan, Jr., argues that Livy must have known the meaning of the word *lingam:* Bayard Taylor had used it in one of his travel books; and "the Victorians seem to have been willing to permit discussion of such 'indelicate' subjects as long as the words themselves were technical or foreign" (339).

was "calculated to subvert morality and encourage unnatural vice," Wilde was questioned sternly about such sentences as "I quite admit that I adored you madly," directed
by one man toward another.[6] And in the summation of
Wilde's second trial, the judge characterized some of the
sentiments expressed in *The Picture of Dorian Gray* as "re-
volting to humanity."[7] Wilde was sentenced to two years in
prison and was released in May 1897, just as Mark Twain,
who was then living in England, was completing *Following
the Equator.* So although it is far from demonstrably the
case, there is reason to suppose that Twain was not just describing a peculiar fruit but was also making a joke for the
attentive. "Fruit," by the way, is moralistically designated
in Eric Partridge's *Dictionary for the Underworld* as having
been a slang term "since before 1933" for "a passive male
degenerate." Given the context, then, Mark Twain's words
are potentially a deliberate double-entendre: "By all accounts, it was a most strange fruit, and incomparably delicious to the taste, but not to the smell. . . . We found many
who had eaten the dorian, and they all spoke of it with a
sort of rapture" (478–79). Homosexual activity was presumably off-limits for Twain, but given his frontier experience, the subject was hardly unknown to him.

On the next page, as Mark Twain describes Benares and
the lingam, the two become fused, and then the dorian re-

6. H. Montgomery Hyde, *Oscar Wilde* (London, 1976), 210,
211.

7. *Ibid.*, 265. Note also that in Twain's story "Hellfire Hotchkiss," the father of a man named Oscar Carpenter says Oscar is "a
girl in disguise. He ought to be put in petticoats" (*S&B*, 178). For
this reason, Hamlin Hill observes that "it is possibly no coincidence in the naming of Oscar that Oscar Wilde's trial and conviction for sodomy had occurred in 1895, two years before the
composition of 'Hellfire Hotchkiss'" (Hamlin Hill, afterword to
Wapping Alice, by Mark Twain [Berkeley, 1981], 77.)

appears. "The site of the town was the beginning-place of the Creation. It was merely an upright 'lingam' at first, no larger than a stove-pipe, and stood in the midst of a shoreless ocean. This was the work of the God Vishnu. Later he spread the lingam out till its surface was ten miles across. Still it was not large enough for the business; therefore he presently built the globe around it. Benares is thus the center of the earth." With Benares and the lingam in effect identical, Twain then devotes the next paragraph to the history and conditions of "it." "It was Buddhist during many centuries—twelve, perhaps—but the Brahmins got the upper hand again, then, and have held it ever since. It is unspeakably sacred in Hindoo eyes, and is as unsanitary as it is sacred, and smells like the rind of the dorian" (480).

Whether this is deliberate play, subterranean association, or mere chance, one can't determine. But it is demonstrable that near the end of the *Equator,* Twain was preoccupied with transsexuality, or at the very least with a blurring of genders. The book's last anecdote concerns an unmarried English military surgeon who built a career in South Africa and India. Somewhat wild as a young man, he had nonetheless become a master at his profession. Moreover, in a duel "he killed his man" (711). A mystery always surrounded him, though. When he died, it was at last revealed that he was a woman. Disgraced in England, she had taken on a new identity in the colonies (712). Such a person existed. Dr. James Barry (1795–1865) was inspector general of the British Army Medical Department. His entry in the *Dictionary of National Biography* observes that "there was a certain effeminacy in his manner which he was always striving to overcome." His case is a seemingly strange note on which to bring a travel book to an end, but hardly out of harmony with Mark Twain's habits. Such confusions of identity attracted him, especially those involving the ambiguities of sex. Well-known instances of transvestism in

Twain's works include Huck dressed as a girl (chaps. 10–11); Tom Driscoll disguised as several women in *Pudd'nhead Wilson,* and his mother Roxy as a man (chaps. 7, 10, 18, 19, 21); and Merlin playing an old peasant woman in *Connecticut Yankee* (chap. 44). Dr. James Barry was but a variant of that aggressive soldier named Joan whose biography Twain had written. In his notebook Twain added: "She (Dr. Barry) was evidently a person of high station. She had been seduced when a girl—as shown on the post mortem. An assumed name. The question is, who was she?"[8]

Sometimes distortions of identity were easily corrected. Once Mark Twain was stopped by an Irish door guard, who asked his name. "Mark Twain." The guard was skeptical: "H'm. H'm. Mike Train. H'm. I don't remember ut" (420). Through cleverness, however, Mark Twain prevailed. In another instance in the *Equator,* a more severe threat was made against his identity. Twain had long suffered, he said, from "lecture-doubles" and had taken legal steps to prevent them from appearing in public and exploiting his reputation (160). One day a letter came for Twain's wife, commiserating with her over the death of her husband in Melbourne at the end of a lecture tour in Australia (159). Since the imposter had apparently died, Twain decided not to pursue the matter, but when he finally reached Australia, he was confounded to learn that the journalists there had never heard of anyone pretending to be him. Only later in the journey did a pleasant, "educated gentleman" confess to having written the make-believe letter of condolence to Mrs. Clemens (244, 250). Moreover, he also admitted to having single-handedly created

8. Notebook no. 38 (May–July 1896), 58, *MTP.* In her dissertation, "Mark Twain's Impostures of Identity" (University of California, Berkeley, 1983), Susan Gillman very usefully analyzes Twain's preoccupation with issues of identity and authenticity.

"the Mark Twain Club of Corrigan Castle, Ireland" (246). This club had initially flattered Twain, then later irritated him because of its incessant flow of questions about his work and requests for his photograph. Now he had met the creator not only of a false death for Twain but also of a false celebrity. These revelations carried with them the enigma of existence. Here a whole enterprise supposedly celebrating Mark Twain's genius had turned out to be not only an irritant but ultimately also an illusion, just like the report of his death. Yet at the time, the perpetrator of the hoax told Twain that creating it had diverted him from thoughts of suicide (249). So had fictions ironically interacted with and affected the lives of both men.

As Mark Twain traveled through the Pacific and into Asia, the local conditions often stimulated his sympathy for the downtrodden. Although the whites had to endure certain infamies during the Indian mutiny, usually the colonized people of other races were abused and hence received Mark Twain's concern. He remembered the abduction of natives from the Pacific island archipelago to work on Australian plantations (81–82). When he actually arrived in Australia, he began to reflect bitterly on the white assumptions of superiority to the "naked skinny aboriginals" and on the various means by which the natives had been exterminated and their land expropriated (207, 211–13). Their treatment struck Twain as "robbery, humiliation, and slow, slow murder" (213). This perception was a clear advance on his part from his old Southern-tainted jokes about miscegenation societies and his fierce contempt toward the American Indians he had encountered in the West. Disillusioned in many respects by the exercise of commercial and political power, and sensitized by the experience of writing first *Huckleberry Finn* and then *Pudd'nhead Wilson*, Twain now easily extended his support to the oppressed.

Moreover, he appreciated their physical beauty and

skills. In Fiji the young girls were "easy and graceful, a pleasure to look at"; the young matrons "incomparable for unconscious stateliness and dignity"; and the young men "majestic" (94). In Ceylon he celebrated "beautiful brown faces, and gracious and graceful gestures and attitudes and movements" (343). In India he observed that "usually the man is a nobly-built great athlete, with not a rag on but his loin-handkerchief," and the woman "a slender and shapely creature, as erect as a lightning-rod" (346). After a time Twain pondered his reactions and concluded that "nearly all black and brown skins are beautiful, but a beautiful white skin is rare" (381). To make his point, he compared the "splendid black satin skin" of the Zulus and the "rich and perfect tint" of the Indians with the complexions of the whites who were "streaming past this London window now" (381, 383). The result he found to be degrading: with one or two exceptions, "sallow," "unwholesome," and "ghastly" were the adjectives that these English faces stimulated in him (382).

After considering the superlative performances of the aboriginal trackers in Australia, he decided that they represented "a craft, a penetration, a luminous sagacity and a minuteness and accuracy of observation" simply not possessed by anyone else (174). It was an encomium he had been reluctant ever to extend to the American Indian. Twain was similarly impressed by the aboriginals' stoicism, and as evidence of it he cited three detailed examples, after warning: "Do not read the following if horrors are not pleasant to you" (219).

Still, the aboriginals did not ultimately seem to be a superior race to Mark Twain, any more than the Europeans or the Polynesians. He reflected thoughtfully on their "freckled" character, quite as mixed and diverse as that of his own tribe (214). Concluding a long list of instances of the extraordinary contradictions of the aboriginal, Twain wrote: "Within certain limits this savage's intellect is the alertest and the brightest known to history or tradition; and yet the poor creature was never able to invent a counting system that would reach above five, nor a vessel that he could boil water in" (215). After accumulating evidence about the treatment of the natives, he concluded: "How glad I am that all these native races are dead and gone, or nearly so. The work was mercifully swift and horrible in some portions of Australia" (256). The methods used by the white invaders revolted Mark Twain whether they involved force or guile, but he conceded, however ironically, their inevitability. Speaking elsewhere of the Australian wild dog, the dingo, he observed: "He had been sentenced to extermination, and the sentence will be carried out. This is all right, and not objectionable. The world was made for man—the white man" (186). Perhaps in an ideal situation things would be otherwise, but as they were not and evidently would never be so, Twain tried to develop an ironic fatalism that could accept things as they were.

Moreover, at least in India, Mark Twain found much to say for English rule as opposed to the absolute and capricious tyranny of various Indian rajahs and princes. The English had eradicated the Thugs (446). They now governed "with apparent ease . . . through tact, training, and distinguished administrative ability, reinforced by just and liberal laws" (518). Further, for all the abuses of conquest that Twain had documented and lamented, his conclusive feeling was that "all the savage lands in the world are going to be brought under subjection to the Christian governments of Europe. I am not sorry, but glad." He was not being ironic. He believed, he wrote, that India demonstrated that after much bloodshed the result would be "peace and order and the reign of law" (625, 626).

Although these hopeful sentiments may have represented Mark Twain's best judgment as he came to the end of his last extensive journey, in fact he would shortly be obliged to repudiate them, and did, with unparalleled indignation, in a series of critiques of imperialistic policy. In 1901 in "To the Person Sitting in Darkness" and "To My Missionary Critics," he addressed hypocritical Christian conversion efforts, especially in China. In 1902 with "In Defense of General Funston," he attacked the American general named and the means by which he put down the Filipino insurrectionaries and captured their leader, Emilio Aguinaldo. And in "King Leopold's Soliloquy" Twain indicted the malign Belgian presence in the Congo. In short, everywhere he looked, that hope for enlightened colonial government expressed in the *Equator* was betrayed by the cruelest oppression and exploitation. In any case, he had hardly been blind to white viciousness before. "There are many humorous things in the world," he said in the *Equator,* "among them the white man's notion that he is less savage than the other savages" (213).

Yet such nihilism was unendurable for him. Mark Twain was many things, not all of them attractive, but he was invariably aroused by suffering and frequently puzzled and distressed by the anomalies of existence. He worked diligently for years to formulate an explanation for the deplorable condition of the world, but he derived neither comfort nor enlightenment from his efforts. As with most of us, escape was at least temporarily preferable. On the way from Ceylon to Mauritius, he said he would prefer never to go ashore again. At sea "there is no weariness, no fatigue, no worry, no responsiblity, no work, no depression of spirits. There is nothing like this serenity, this comfort, this peace, this deep contentment, to be found anywhere on land. If I had my way I would sail on forever and never go to live on the solid ground again" (617). Such sentiments he had once invested in raft life: separation from trouble, going nowhere perpetually, ever drifting.

Few alternatives occurred to him. Once in India he watched an artist who made pictures by sprinkling colored dust on water. Seeing a creation so ephemeral that a breath could destroy it, Twain reflected that finally all men's monuments and temples were no more than this—"water pictures." The dust image struck him as "a sermon, an allegory, a symbol of Instability" (505). But despite the validity of this perception and the truly heroic efforts he made to adjust to this capitalized instability, he himself was never afforded the gift of balance, of following an equator of equanimity. He could only counter the perceived injustices of this world with the humanity of his indignation, and of his laughter.

8

A fragment originally intended for *Following the Equator* captures some of the bewildered frustration of Mark Twain's sixties. It describes "The Enchanted Sea-Wilderness," also known as "the Devil's Race-Track" and "the Everlasting Sunday." It was one of those fabled regions in the ocean where mariners are becalmed, and by extension it suggests a psychic state of motionless despair, only here no albatross has been shot. The curse is arbitrary. It constitutes "a trap," a place of "horrible stillness," whose prisoners suffer a "profound inertness," a "universal paralysis of life and energy" (*WWD*, 81–82). Such areas, or mental states, Twain calls "spots and patches where no compass has any value. When the compass enters one of these bewitched domains it goes insane and whirls this way and that and settles nowhere, and is scared and distressed, and cannot be comforted" (76).

Early in Twain's work, guides had misled their charges through venality and ignorance; here some larger breakdown of natural law was involved. At the same time, by attributing human suffering to the disoriented compass, Twain suggests that it too is part of the human psyche. We are told that the compass "acted like a frightened thing, a thing in frantic fear for its life. And so we got afraid of it, and could not bear to look at its distress and its helpless struggles; for we came to believe that it had a soul and that it was in hell" (82–83).

The implications of Twain's perspective here are so problematic that, unable to control this narrative, he eventually abandoned it. Whatever his difficulties in managing it, though, with that image of the compass in total distress and incapable of pointing accurately, Twain had created a powerful image of confusion so complete that it caused frantic torment in the agent responsible for providing direction and appalled paralysis among those dependent on its guidance. Twain breaks off the narrative approximately where he found himself in the mid-1890s: "When the men began to starve and die they were   " (86).

A lifetime's accumulated frustration did not, however, quell Mark Twain's search for understanding. If travel under normal conditions in this world failed to bring enlightenment, then his imagination created other worlds and other viewpoints from which to ponder them. In an 1898 notebook, he made this entry: "Aug. 10. Last night dreamed of a whaling cruise in a drop of water" (*MTN*, 365). This note expanded into another of his extended fragments, "The Great Dark." In it the narrator, after looking through a microscope at a drop of "stale water from a puddle in the carriage-house" and seeing various monstrous creatures swimming in it, begins to reflect on this sight: "An ocean in a drop of water—and unknown, uncharted, unexplored by man! By man, who gives all his time to the Africas and the poles, with this unsearched marvelous world right at his elbow" (*WWD*, 104).

Having conceived this situation, Mark Twain could not bring it under control either. John S. Tuckey's analyses show the various strategies Twain tried before finally giving up altogether on the project (*WWD*, 15–20, 99–101). One of these involved the narrator's meeting a stranger on board ship who says the others call him "The Mad Passenger," although, he adds: "O dear, think of the irony of it—they call me mad—*they!* Do you know what these people are doing. They've got a chart of *Dreamland,* and they are navigating this ship by it!" (561).

If the world of mental delusion intrigued Mark Twain, he was not prepared to engage it further, so he dropped "The Mad Passenger" section from "The Great Dark" and turned to elaborate its dream aspect. The narrator falls into conversation with "the Superintendent of Dreams" while on the ship. Eventually, in some heat, he tells the Superintendent: "If my style doesn't suit you, you can end the dream as soon as you please—right now, if you like." This exchange then ensues:

> "The dream? *Are you quite sure it is a dream?*"
> It took my breath away.
> "What do you mean? Isn't it a dream?"
> He looked at me in that same way again, and it made my blood chilly, this time. Then he said—
> "You have spent your whole life in this ship. And this is *real* life. Your other life was the dream!"
>
> (*WWD,* 124)

Although this narrative too finally goes nowhere, we can see that it, like Twain's other fragmentary conceptions, dramatizes a possible explanation for the precarious instability of human understanding. One is suddenly becalmed where a compass is of no use, whereupon a state of inertness ensues. Or one is mad. Or "they" are. Or what one has taken for a dream turns out to be reality. As none of these strategies gained anything resembling permanent acceptance from Twain, it should not surprise us to find him yielding at times to nihilism. Having long pondered, without resolution, the meaning of what he had observed in his travels through the world, Twain told his old friend and clergyman Joe Twichell, in a letter of July 28, 1904, that at least "a *part* of each day—or night" the world vanished absolutely for him, leaving him no more than a thought drifting aimlessly in emptiness. At such moments it seemed to him that everything was "NON–EXISTENT. That is, that there is *nothing*. That there is no God and no universe; that there is only empty space, and in it a lost and homeless and wandering and companionless and indestructible *Thought*. And I am that thought" (*MSM,* 30).

That thought could not cancel existence, though, so Mark Twain's travels were far from over. Perpetual movement seemed the answer to the precariousness of life. He moved to keep from sinking. From 1899 forward, he went to Vienna, to Budapest, to Prague, to Cologne, to London, to Sweden, to London, to Manhattan, to Saranac Lake, to Nova Scotia, to the West Indies, to Hannibal, to Maine. It was now 1903. He crossed the Atlantic again to Genoa, Italy, went up to Florence, then back to Elmira, New York, to Massachusetts, to Manhattan, to New Hampshire. From 1906: when at home, he paced relentlessly round and round his billiard table, gratefully calculating the perfectly straight lines and angles for the perfectly round balls. "The games begin right after luncheons, daily, & continue until midnight, with 2 hours' intermission for dinner & music. And so it is 9 hours exercise per day & 10 or 12 on Sunday" (*MTB,* 1327). Off again to Bermuda, to London, to Oxford, back to Tuxedo, New York, to Bermuda, to Connecticut. To Bermuda. Then he was carried in a deck chair, a ship's berth, an invalid carriage, and a compartment on the afternoon express, back to Connecticut. There at last in 1910 at his villa, Stormfield, his travels stopped.

Index

Compositor: G&S Typesetters, Inc.
Printer: Thomson-Shore
Binder: John H. Dekker & Sons
Text: 10/12 Bembo
Display: Bembo